FLORIDA FABLES

The Story of

THE SARASOTA CELERY FIELDS
And Other Mysteries

A Novel

FLORIDA FABLES

The Story of

THE SARASOTA CELERY FIELDS
And Other Mysteries

TONY DUNBAR

Blind Pass Publications
Florida

*Harry L. Higel, beloved civic leader and three time mayor
of Sarasota. Brutally slain on Siesta Key in 1921.*

Blind Pass Publications, LLC
Post Office Box 1096
Englewood, FL 34295

Credit for the photograph on page 60: "Convicts leased to harvest timber,"
State Archives of Florida, Florida Memory, Image RC12880

PROMISE

This story is about fifty percent true.

DEDICATION

Nancy,

No other light shall guide my steps

Than the sparkle of you, coming into sight

– Robert Burns

The Story of
THE SARASOTA CELERY FIELDS
And Other Mysteries

A NOVEL

It all changed so fast.

My name is Gawain MacFarlane, though people have started calling me Gabe. I call myself white, but I was raised among the Ephrams, a Black family. Back then people were more understanding of these sort of arrangements. Of course, there were fewer people then, too. I am speaking of the days when Southwest Florida was still a frontier, full of wild cattle and bears, back when in autumn sea turtles were thick on the beach and people lived on what they could scrounge from our sandy soil or gather from unspoiled nature. Black people called whites "Sir," when they were in town, but not necessarily when they were out in the country, which was where we lived. Nobody called me anything but Gawain, or "boy," or "son" around our house.

In fact, I'd call Mr. Ephram "Sir." Not the other way around. Even after I grew up, I always called him Mister. Today you can't do that. There's so much hatred now. I'd be run out of Sarasota if I was heard calling him or any other colored man "Mister," and if he called me by my given name, Gawain or Gabe, where people could hear, why he'd be flogged and maybe hung.

And there was a Mrs. Ephram, Cordelia, who made me my supper.

She looked after me, and was the most mother I had. My living quarters were in the stables.

The reason Missus Cordelia looked after me and the reason I was raised in a barn are related. First off, my own mother, Penny MacFarlane, died bringing me into the world, so I never did know her. Second, my father, Wallace MacFarlane, died in a house fire when I was only four. He had been a cavalryman fighting Yankees all over Tennessee with his two best friends, Captain Duff and Sandy Watson. They were like The Three Musketeers, those men. My father was grievously wounded in the war.

After my dad perished in the fire, Mr. Sandy Watson took me in, but he had me reside on his citrus farm in the country – away from his own wife and children. Since I've been an adult I've had the growing suspicion that Mr. Watson was my real father, partly because the nature of the wounds Wallace MacFarlane sustained in the war might have prevented him from conceiving me and partly because Mr. Watson seemed to want to keep me close, but not too close. So I was raised among the Ephrams on an orange farm in the country, in the stables. That may sound like a sorry upbringing, but it wasn't bad at all.

I had the groves to get lost in. I had the woods and all their creatures, day and night. I learned about firearms, knives, hunting and trapping. I kept a snake collection. I learned all about plants, wild and tame. I had many nice Florida evenings just watching the sun slip down behind the pines while the livestock snorted and lowed and the owls hooted good night. But most of all, I had the love and guidance of the first real family I ever knew, the Ephrams.

Just about the time I turned eighteen I left the Watson place and undertook my famous ride to hunt down Charley Willard, the dumbest "assassin" in the "Sarasota Assassination Society."

Charley was a brute, and had a mental capacity that made shooting the Federal Postmaster, the most prominent man in town, in broad daylight, with an eye-witness present, seem like a good thing to do. He was a hell of a renegade though, and dragged me through half of south Florida until his toes were worn to stubs, his tongue was black, and we were both near-delirious. But I ran him to ground. That capture was big news in Sarasota and all around. It made my reputation and changed my life.

Now I've taken a seat to write down all of this. The question is why. One reason is that I've reached the point in life where I want to remember my wins. There have been a lot of them, I'm proud to say. Another reason is that I've been preparing to write stories ever since I was old enough to wash my own dishes. I read somewhere, Jack London I think, that you could become a writer if you learned three new words a day. I took that to heart and for many a year pulled out the Webster's most nights after supper was cleared away, while I settled in to relax myself with a cup of coffee. Fortunately, my stories about growing up in Florida, wearing a badge and taming our own Wild West, turned out to be worth reading, in my opinion.

Of course, my life was not just full of "wins." Another reason for doing this is that I want to write down the things I know caused pain to me and others. I suppose I need to explain myself to myself. To be honest you've got to take the bitter with the sweet, yes? And in our golden city of Sarasota, with its lovely weather and its splendid sunrises and sparkling sunsets, it's hard to dwell upon the bitter. So, please don't. Before I die, I'm planning to toss those pages in the fire and drink a toast while they burn. So, let's begin.

TABLE OF CONTENTS

CHAPTER ONE

I BECAME A MARSHAL

Right about 1895, maybe a little earlier, I was appointed Constable of the town of Sarasota, Florida, a job which lasted about seven years. Then, all of a sudden because Sarasota was growing so fast, they decided they needed a city council, and the city council decided they needed a City Marshal, so that became my new title. As City Marshal, I automatically became a Deputy Sheriff of Manatee County, and here's where my career as a lawman really began.

Even at the start, our boom town needed more law than any one man could give it. Busting heads all by myself was dangerous and taxing. With hotel construction, new houses, fish camps, and construction workers rolling in, I was mostly breaking up fights and dealing with bootleggers, many of whom I knew. It was often necessary to make accommodations since I didn't want to come home stretched out on a plank. Even so, I got into plenty of scrapes and my wife Clarinda complained loudly about stitching me up.

Every marshal needs a deputy, so I hired my lifetime buddy Reuben Ephram who had been working around Clarinda's and my farm as a hired hand.

Let me tell you about Reuben. Reuben was and still is more than a little bit crazy. Like me, he was raised by the Ephrams, but he actually lived in their house, not in the barn. He appeared as white as me, and Mr. Ephram called him a "foundling," whatever that is. Reuben was just past my age, but way bigger and better looking than me, and he liked to laugh, fight, hunt coons at night, whistle at the girls, and, before Mr. Ephram caught him at it, make moonshine.

Reuben was the one who'd save your pig or your baby from a wolf or alligator, but not the one you'd nominate for the church choir, though he did have a good voice. Clarinda cared for him – Reuben is hard not to like - but she was never keen having him around our place on a permanent basis. She didn't mind it a bit, and it probably helped our marriage, when he finally moved out.

Where Reuben came from was always a mystery, but now I think I've figured it out. I'll get to that later.

Clarinda took up church work and formed quite a society around our Catfish Creek community, were we lived on a small farm with goats, cows, horses, chickens and dogs. It took many years, ten about, but finally Clarinda and I had a child. His name is Wallace MacFarlane, too, just like my dad, but we always called the boy Mack.

Sawmills and turpentine stills were coming into the county by then, and so did Mrs. Bertha Palmer, buying up land everywhere she could. The Celery Fields got opened up, and soon there were labor camps all over the countryside, but they were outside my jurisdiction.

I only got involved on the weekends, when the workers were brought into town to shop and enjoy their meager amount of time away from work. Black communities called Overtown and Newtown sprang up on the outskirts of Sarasota proper.

We got roads, and then we got Tin Can Tourists. They rolled in by the thousands in their new Model T's to see our sunny beaches and pick oranges by the trunk-load. We got a railroad right to Main Street in Sarasota. The Seaboard Air Line Railway, "Straight as a Plumb Line to the Winter Resorts of Florida." Everything in sight was for sale – house lots, "grove" lots, half-an-acre farms, swamp land needing only a "little" drainage work, property that would "surely soon be reached" by a road, mangrove islands in Sarasota Bay. And for a long time, everything sold.

My father's old Confederate States of America Cavalry buddy, Captain Duff, was elected Manatee County Sheriff, based in large part on the role he had played in capturing the ringleaders of the "Sarasota Assassination Society" – just as my appointments as constable and marshal were due mainly to my part in bringing them to justice. Also, Duff was ready to take on the "big boys," the land scammers, what they now call "developers," who were developing the countryside by burning out all of the pioneers. The scammers considered these poor hard-working people to be illegal cracker squatters whose removal was necessary so that the scammers could obtain huge chunks of the county for themselves. I saw all of this going on. Everybody did. But there was not a whole lot anybody could do.

Not surprisingly, Captain Duff did not last long as sheriff. He was ousted after one term by Jasper Braxton's faction; Braxton being the main land scammer. The Captain went back to milling lumber, which he was good at, and he prospered, despite the attempts early on by the Braxton boys to sabotage his business. Politics has always been taken seriously in our neck of the woods.

I drifted away from Sandy Watson, the Ephrams' landlord who was the sheriff before Captain Duff. He never would admit to me that I was his son, and his silence made a rift between us that has not been healed. He's past 70 now. It doesn't seem possible that he's so old, just as it's hard to believe how old I'm getting. I guess I'm lucky to be here at all. I can still outwork any man in the county.

That's the big picture, but I'll take a step back and go a little slower. Let's see if I can put my stories down in more or less the same order they happened. Fair Warning! They aren't all pretty and a lot of them involve meanness, greed and a significant amount of violence! But that was how Sarasota was back then, pretty on the outside with an underbelly that wasn't quite so attractive.

CHAPTER TWO

BREAKING UP STILLS

Not long after I became town Constable the Spanish War kicked off. Though we were all against it initially, community sentiment changed when it was learned that Tampa would be the port of disembarkation for the whole United States Army. Before you could blink, about 40,000 soldiers and 10,000 bootleggers arrived in Tampa. Our little, home-town whiskey peddlers down here in Sarasota and even further south saw this as an opportunity to grow up and sell lots more booze. The soldiers demanded barrels of sauce, and stills popped up everywhere from old Myakka City to Arcadia to Englewood and all points in between.

I hardly cared about breaking up stills, but at that time it became the principal occupation of law enforcement, and I was the only law south of Manatee City, which is now what they've decided to call Bradenton, and north of Punta Gorda and Charlotte Harbor. That's a lot of territory. The better elements of the Sarasota community expected me to do something about the illegal predilection of men to drink alcohol and the greed of those who supplied the means for their evil habit. So, of course, I did; even though those same "better elements" did a fair amount of tippling themselves.

The rowdiness of a certain element who drink too much is something you expect to go with the job, and I had my hands full running drunk cowboys and fishermen off the streets until most of them finally got the message. And the message was, take your booze to the south side of town where there were plenty of illicit honky-tonks, or take it out to the country by Phillippi Creek where there were popular joints set discreetly back in the pine trees, or take it anywhere you want, but don't take it to Main Street or Cunliff Lane or anywhere the "decent" folk have to see you. Most of the cowboy boozers went along with the plan as easy as you please so long as they could see straight enough to focus on my badge and my gun. I only had to slap around the ones who were blind drunk, which I could do then because I was young and a hard man to put down. I never did have to shoot anybody. What sticks in my memory is being asked basically to tame a wilderness.

To tell the truth, I didn't really believe it needed to be tamed. I kind of enjoyed the rough and rugged way it was then, but when I was called upon by respectable townsfolk to clamp down on one of those back-alley or dirt-road saloons, I had to get a little more business-like. Of course, you can't walk into a joint full of paying, boozed-up customers, even if you have a deputy like Reuben along, and expect the proprietor to lock the door and everybody to leave their drinks on the bar and go home just because you tell them to. That's why you have to make those accommodations. You have to meet with the master or mistress of the place one-on-one, preferably outside of normal business hours. That usually means the narrow window from the middle of the morning, after everybody's had their breakfast to quiet their stomachs and before noon when some fellows want to drink their lunch. It was the routine of police work in those days.

The owner I remember best was a big tall woman, Beatrice Flower, or "Footsie" they called her, who had a place tucked away in the woods off a farm road, what they now call Cattlemen. She lived in her little house parked in a pine grove in back of her rustic joint, and I caught her on her porch-swing asleep. I could hear someone doing the dishes inside. At the foot of the steps I cleared my throat loudly, and she woke up.

"Hello, Constable MacFarlane," she said dreamily, and smiled. That's the kind of welcome you look for. Footsie wasn't a bad looking woman, even first thing in the morning, according to her clock, before she rouged up; she had long yellow hair and high cheekbones and an erect bearing that men found attractive. When she was working she could swear like a teamster as the occasion required and had no qualms about hauling out the peacemaker she stored behind the bar if her authority was questioned, which it rarely was. I knew her good points because I had stepped into her place when duty called me into that particular neighborhood, and we had gotten to know each other in a friendly way.

So we chatted for a minute and she invited me to join her on the porch. The screen door opened part way and a young woman looked out, checking on things, but Footsie waved her off.

I sat down on the swing and explained that there had been complaints from some of the preachers in the area who had gotten their deacons, three of them, to ride into Sarasota and express their congregations' dismay about Miss Flower's operation and desire that it be shut down forthwith.

"Is blackmail an option?" she asked.

I told her I didn't know what that was supposed to mean, and she named one of the pastors and claimed to have personally delivered packaged goods to the big pepper bush planted at the entrance to his parsonage driveway.

"I suppose blackmail is something you might consider," I said, "but what I had in mind was you making some financial contributions to their church building funds and shutting down your business for a month or two."

"And making a financial contribution to you?"

"Now that won't be necessary, Beatrice, but what you might want to do is walk into church on Sunday morning and when the preacher makes the call, go right up to the pulpit and be saved."

She laughed, and I thought that would be the end of it. I told her she had to close up, except maybe for a few personal friends who would blow out their brains if they were cut off, at least until October, which was two months off, when the farmers went back to work and would be too busy to worry about community sin.

"Or you'll do what?" she asked, serious now.

"If you stay open I will have to get a court order, and the sheriff will come down here from Bradenton with a whole bunch of deputies and close this business of yours up for good."

She stood up, straightened her dress, and said, "Maybe I do need salvation, not that it's any of your business, but we're done talking." I tipped my hat and got back on my horse. (This was before Mr. Ford). She went into her house and slammed the screen door behind her.

I had no reason to expect anything good to come out of this conversation, but it did. Footsie acted on my advice, and the very next Sunday she got herself saved at the Garden of Gethsemane True Baptist Fellowship, and she closed her bar down. She converted it into a rib shack called "Miss Flower's Wayside Inn," and got a new clientele, and most of her old ones came back, too. I think she sold a few bottles, maybe even shots, in her back room to folks she knew well, but I never said anything and never heard another bad word about her.

As for all the stills that were springing up in the county, to me it was just more of the same old line of business that had let the poor settlers make a few dollars in wilderness days. The county had always been legally dry, even way before Prohibition, but that had never made much difference that I could see. There had always been plenty of cookers around that could be broken up if that's what a cop wanted to do. To be honest, as long as the folks involved were all local, and kept their doings out of the public eye, my policy was to look the other way. Poor people need to make a living just as much as you and I.

As a result, and unlike lots of other lawmen around the state, I did not make a reputation out of smashing drums of moonshine. Most of my constituents in Sarasota never seemed to mind booze much unless it was flaunted in a way that couldn't be ignored. One such encounter comes to my mind. The only reason I had to go after this particular operation was because it was built by a son of a bitch named Jerome Powers and it was behind his run-down trashy cabin right where Cunliff Lane ended at that time. Now, Cunliff was turning into a fashionable street and people, the same people who signed my paycheck, knew about the still, they could even smell it when the wind was right, and they wanted it gone.

I explained this to Jerome as best I could, right in the woods while he was cooking mash. I had Reuben, my deputy, with me.

"Jerome, you dumb bastard!" I yelled. "What are you doing making liquor right here in the middle of town?"

He didn't even bother to frame an answer. He just grabbed a stick of firewood as long as his arm and charged, swinging it at my head. Reuben had the presence of mind to stick out his boot and trip the man, and he hit the ground spread-eagled right at my feet. I tore the piece of firewood from his hands and whapped him until he was out. Reuben had some cuffs, which was good because Jerome was still belligerent when he came to, and it required some effort to get him to hike out from the trees.

I went and borrowed an axe from Jake Adams who had a house going up nearby, and I used it to bust the pot up good. The mash poured out over the fire and put it out. I yanked off the copper coil for evidence and returned the axe.

Jerome did ten days in jail and was fined $10, but I don't know if he ever paid it. He put his place up for sale and moved away. He probably made good money out of the transaction since I doubt he paid anything for his lot to begin with.

CHAPTER THREE

THE FATE OF CHARLEY WILLARD

When Captain Duff was County Sheriff and I was the Sarasota City Marshal, there was one highlight that outshone all the others. I got to preside over the death of Charley Willard, the cold-blooded killer who murdered our poor postmaster, Mr. Abbe. This is how Charley finally got what was coming to him.

Some twenty years before, I had captured Charley and brought him in for trial. Like I said earlier, it was a feat that made my reputation. Charley was sentenced to life, but after spending four years as a lease-labor convict in the state prison camp near Live Oak he escaped, not to be seen again. This is how dumb and unlucky Charley was - a year after he escaped the rest of the bunch were pardoned – due to political corruption. They were set free! But because of his escape, Charley was a wanted man.

Now, Sheriff Duff didn't drink liquor himself, but he was tolerant of it. He was also highly tolerant of voters, and those voters who made the most noise about liquor were not the drinkers. The drinkers were a large constituency for sure but, nevertheless, they were scofflaws in a dry county and unlikely ever to go to the polls. No, the truly noisy voters were the "prohibitionists." We had a lively Anti-Saloon League in the county and, of course, an enthusiastic Women's Christian Temperance Union, which my Clarinda took an interest in. (Though women couldn't actually cast ballots back then, they had a lot of sway with those who did.)

In about 1910, the combined teetotalers held a big "Barbecue and Prohibition Rally" on the bridge across the Manatee river at Bradenton. They brought in national speakers, and all the local dignitaries were there. A captain of the Army musicians, one J.C. Johnson, brought the United States Military Band over from Fort Dade. The bridge was closed to traffic for the event, and it was free to the public. But out at the fringes of this big community affair was where the real action was taking place.

I went, wearing Sunday clothes and my badge and my gun, but they were for show. I had no expectation of trouble. Clarinda was along, and so was our son Mack, then about ten years-old. We could pass through the crowd easily since I was an official, and we found Captain Duff, dressed in a sober black suit and his trademark pearl gray Homburg, right in front of the bandstand, shaking hands and showing off his handle-bar mustaches. Nobody ever looked more like a county sheriff than Lionel Duff. His downfall was that he wouldn't kiss the right asses. But on this sunny day we said our hellos, slapped some backs, and watched the band getting set to play. They were a nice looking bunch in their Army uniforms, with their dark blue dress coats and sky-blue trousers.

In the midst of these festivities I heard what I thought was a gunshot back on the riverside, where there were old docks and commercial buildings. Sheriff Duff heard it, too, and frowned. I could see he was torn between forcing his way back through the crowd to investigate and staying put and politicking. I sighed. At that time he was, after all, my boss and the man I respected and listened to more than any other.

Reluctantly, I nodded at my sheriff, told Clarinda I'd be right back, and squeezed my way through all the people, saying excuse me and sorry, until I had cleared the main part of the crowd. There was a part of town there called "under the bridge," though it extended a block or two in either direction on the street that runs alongside the river.

On this particular day, I didn't imagine there were too many vagabonds or rowdies actually under the bridge, where I knew games of chance and opportunities for vice often abounded, but there were low-class grub-joints and private saloons catering to working men in between some of the respectable merchant establishments up and down the street. The latter were closed today, but there was the sound of loud voices coming from one of the low wooden buildings with its windows painted black and no advertisement out front. Rather than knock, I walked in and closed the door behind me.

The shouts and loud arguments didn't stop just because I was there, and when my eyes adjusted to the dim light I could make out a rude counter where glasses of drink had been poured but set aside due to some sort of altercation. A table and chairs had been overturned, and I could see playing cards and coins had been strewn about the floor. I had stepped into the middle of something deadly serious.

A circle of men had faced off around the table. Two were showing pistols and one was showing a knife. Sitting on the floor clutching his stomach was a bearded fisherman wearing a red plaid shirt which was getting redder from his own blood. The situation became clear mighty fast.

"Hold on!" I yelled, and got a little attention.

"I'm Deputy Sheriff MacFarlane! Everybody holster them weapons and step back from that table!"

There was no immediate compliance so I lifted the gun out of my holster in slow motion and pointed it at all of them, one at the time. My nerves got quite a jolt when my eyes fell on the third man in line. He was Charley Willard, the killer from the old Sarasota Assassination Society, whom I had famously arrested and brought to justice. I knew him, and he knew me.

"Gawain MacFarlane! You son of a bitch!" was what he managed to say.

"Willard! You're wanted for murder!" I yelled right as he was jumping for cover over the counter, pistol in hand.

And he raised that hand over the bar to fire a wild shot right over my head that blasted a hole in the front wall of the store, which sadly let in enough sunlight that he could see me even better.

All the other bad gentlemen scurried to their various corners pointing at me and each other with their weapons, while the bleeding man on the floor began to wail and crawl in my direction, I guess to get out the door. I was in a bad place and threw myself onto the planks, crawling through the dust and grime to try to get my eyes behind the bar so I could see that bastard Willard and shoot him. Somebody else fired off his gun and put a bullet into the wall right above my left eyeball.

And what I think happened next is that Willard vaulted back across the bar and made a run for it, jumping right over me and racing out the door. Anyway, I saw the blur, almost smelled the man, heard his boots pound the floor, was blinded by the flash of light when he broke out of the door, and then heard two gunshots.

I rolled onto my knees and leapt outside, and there was Charley Willard splayed out on the sidewalk, and there was Captain Duff with his service revolver, half in a squat, frozen.

Slowly, he stood erect. "Ain't done that in a while," he said. A crowd was running up. Willard was dead, one bullet to his forehead, right between his black bushy eyebrows, and the other was to his chest, where his shirt was staining red. All I could say was, "Damn!" The men from inside the saloon slipped behind me and drifted away as fast as they could down the street. I remember that the military band was playing the "Miss Liberty March" up on the bridge. The man who had been on the floor crawled out last and limped away holding his belly.

I went up to hug Captain Duff and started laughing. I couldn't help it. And in a moment he started laughing, too. But quickly, he caught himself, imagining how it might look. But not me. I just sat back in the doorway of that bar and had a good time laughing. Charley had finally met justice, while I had narrowly escaped an untimely death.

And through no fault of my own, I still had my record of never shooting a man.

Nobody claimed Charley Willard's body.

CHAPTER FOUR

THE JOHN ASHLEY GANG

Some things happen very strangely in this world. Willard was not my last run in with members of the Sarasota Assassination Society, and that brings me around to my chance encounter with the John Ashley Gang. This would have been in 1915. Now, we thought we were booming over here on the West Coast of Florida, but on the East Coast, the Atlantic side, the boom had been booming for twenty years. We didn't know it then, but we know it now. To this day we are still twenty years behind that side of the state. But anyway, with all of that money flowing over there, the conditions were ripe for ruthless men to take advantages.

I had first heard about the Ashley family when I was in the Caloosahatchee River area on the trail of Charley Willard. The Ashleys were poor farmers then. Later I heard that the father of the clan had moved the family to the East Coast looking for railroad work and then somehow got elected sheriff over in West Palm Beach. Though he didn't serve long.

His son, John Ashley, took a different route, engaging in a variety of crimes. For a while he was a rum runner, picking up the bottled whiskey that was being smuggled in by the boatload from Barbados and distributing it to customers north of the Everglades. Then he partnered with a Seminole Indian trapping otters for their skins. John murdered his partner and took the hides, which he then sold for $1,100, good money. He was arrested for the murder of the Seminole, but he escaped from custody.

John was a resourceful criminal if nothing else. On the run and wanted for murder, he joined up with his brothers and some Chicago gangsters, and they became the Ashley Gang. They were blamed for all manner of crimes around the whole of south Florida, and even as far north as Jacksonville. They tried, but failed, to rob a train on the East Coast, and that made some news. Then they successfully robbed a bank in Stuart. I knew about the robbery one day after it happened because it was the front page story in newspapers all over the state. As the desperados were leaving the Stuart bank with their $4,000 of loot, one of the "Gang" managed to shoot his own chief in the face. John was blinded and bleeding and needing medical attention. Brother Bill got his wounded leader to a woods hideaway and stayed with him while Brother Bob went in search of a doctor. According to the papers, the doctor Bob did find absolutely refused to ride out to the camp. But the Palm Beach County Sheriff, George B. Baker, somehow got wind of this and where John was hiding and went with a posse to capture him, which they did, and carted him off to jail. I learned later that the medical staff removed his busted eye. At first John declined to have a glass eye fitted because he figured he was going to be hung anyway for killing the Indian, but he was acquitted. Later on, he got that glass eye.

Anyhow, as I said, the reason I knew about the Stuart bank robbery was because the newspapers treated it like a big sensation, and in one story there was a photograph of the doctor who had refused to treat John Ashley, and the more I studied it, the more he looked like Dr. Leonard Andrews.

Now, Dr. Andrews was one of the main Sarasota "assassins" though he didn't do the killing. He was just a superior white Midwesterner who gave the orders for his stupid Florida-born disciples to act on. The trial judge and jury took unkindly to this and sentenced him to be hung. However, due to the miserable state of affairs at the Pine Level jail, including the susceptibility of the jailer to be bribed, the doctor climbed down a ladder and escaped, never to be found again. Ed Bacon, one of our local Sarasota boys who truly enjoyed the work of killing, ran off with him.

Now, twenty-five years later, here was a picture of that very same Dr. Andrews, living in Stuart on the Atlantic shoreline, directly across the state from Sarasota.

We had good telephone service by that time, and I called up our new county sheriff, Josiah Gates, who was officially my boss though the Sarasota city council really paid me. (This was after Captain Duff was out of office.) I reported this great revelation about Dr. Andrews, but the sheriff was not impressed. Sheriff Gates' main political attribute was that he was a big man. And his main virtue was that he left Sarasota to me. He was angling for a job as State Prison Inspector, where he would have endless opportunities for graft, and I suspect he had no interest in interrupting his travels about the state, trading patronage, to embark on a dangerous mission to arrest a wicked but forgotten killer. Three-fourths of his constituents had not even lived in Florida back when the brutal assassinations were committed. Also, the few locals who remembered the murders, at least some of them, had come to associate the ringleader Andrews as a persecuted champion of the Democratic Party and its crusade to "redeem" the state from the Republicans. This is a distortion of history, but so be it.

Sheriff Josiah Gates did, however, award me $20 for expenses if I was determined to go. He said he would call Sheriff Baker over in West Palm Beach and tell him I was on the way.

I immediately packed my bag, collected deputy Reuben Ephram and crammed a trunkload of firearms in the boot of the official city car I got to drive. It would be a couple more years before I could afford a vehicle of my own.

Just as I was about to lock up my office, the phone rang and it was Gates again, and I think I remember near-about exactly how he put it.

"I just spoke to Sheriff Baker and he says you are to lay off the doctor. He says that doctor's name is Busby, and he has an excellent reputation. He is not named Andrews. Baker insists that Dr. Busby is a loyal supporter, and Busby's driver is the one who tipped off Sheriff Baker as to where John Ashley was hiding in the woods. In other words, drop the case!"

Five minutes later I was on the road with Reuben. It took us most of the day to get as far as Okeechobee, where we ate a hot greasy meal at a roadhouse and bedded down in the car. Well before dawn we were rolling again and got to Stuart, after a ferry ride across the St. Lucie River, in time for breakfast. We inquired of the waitress who served us our ham and eggs where a Dr. Busby might be found. It turned out that he would be found at his pineapple farm outside of a village they called Palm City which we had driven through an hour before. We had to take the car ferry back across the St. Lucie, which took some time. It was after noon, due to further stops to ask directions, when we reached a driveway off a long dirt road and a mailbox marked "Doctor."

We pulled over there to arm ourselves, and while we were so occupied another car came racing down the road behind us and, spattering gravel, made a sliding turn into the driveway and disappeared in the dust.

"I don't know who that was," Reuben said, "but I'm ready if you are."

I nodded. Sure, I was ready! We drove in after the car, only going slow. We came quietly upon the garden and then the house, where there were two cars outside. I parked alongside them, and just as we were beginning to get out, the front door of the house burst open and we found ourselves smack in the thick of a gun battle. A large man with a fedora hat backed out of the doorway and was immediately blown into the yard by a shotgun blast to his chest. He fell like a tree dropping in the river. The fellow holding that shotgun appeared in the doorway. He took one look at us and fired at Reuben, which got him in the upper part of his left thigh. As Reuben went down he fired back with the Colt

.45 he was holding and punched a hole in the man's head. Reuben was a good shot, even wounded. He put another slug in the man's chest. As my deputy was keeling over in pain, another car careened in behind us, and men waving badges and shotguns piled out.

Reuben and I both stood down. He actually sat down to tend to his bleeding thigh. I put both my hands, one holding a sawed-off .12 gauge, in the air as high as I could.

The local sheriff, Sheriff Baker, took in the situation and asked my name. I told him, and he said I could put my hands down. He wasn't too pleased about me being in his jurisdiction after having expressly said I was to stay away, but he had two dead men to investigate.

Using his boot, Baker flipped over the fellow on the porch whom Reuben had slain. He knew him. "That's Joe Drake," he said sadly, "the man who fingered John Ashley's hideout." I knew that man, too. "That's Ed Bacon," I corrected him. "A murdering son of a bitch who was condemned to die. His sentence has now been carried out."

Sheriff Baker didn't look convinced. He just spat out an oath and examined the other dead body, the one who had been knocked off the porch onto the ground. This corpse had a bushy beard which somehow I hadn't noticed in the one second I saw him alive. I didn't recognize him. Sheriff Baker next entered the house with his deputy on his heels, guns drawn. Reuben was getting his bleeding under control with a handkerchief for a tourniquet and motioned for me that he was okay. So I went inside, too.

An old man was sitting on the sofa in the front parlor. He had a sheet wrapped around his knees and there was a pillow propped up against the armrest. He had probably been lying down when all of the commotion started. It was Dr. Leonard Andrews, and he didn't look well. Drained out by all of his hatefulness, I thought. The sheriff was talking to him in low tones. Then Baker noticed me listening in behind him and ordered me to go outside and wait.

I did as told. Eventually the peace officers emerged, and we started sorting everything out.

The man on the ground, whose chest the murderer, Ed Bacon, had parted was Bob Ashley, the Ashley gang leader's brother. He had evidently come to seek revenge on whoever had ratted out his brother John. Sheriff Baker knew Ed Bacon as Joe Drake. He was a petty criminal and drug addict but was a reliable snitch for law enforcement and driver for the doctor. The man the sheriff knew as Dr. Busby, and who was "off limits," was a member of the sheriff's church and was far too frail to deal with my false and slanderous accusations and mistaken identification.

Sheriff Baker suggested he might lock Reuben up for killing Ed Bacon, but elementary crime reasoning made it pretty obvious who shot who first. Either of Reuben's bullets would have instantly killed Bacon and that would have given him no time to fire the shot that hit Reuben. So Bacon had to have shot first.

It was also quite clear that I was not going to be permitted to leave the area with Dr. Andrews, but to tell the truth I didn't have the heart to take him with me. He looked so sick and harmless. I was quite satisfied, however, to see Ed Bacon, another member of the Sarasota

23

Assassination Society, dead. And I was relieved to help Reuben into the car and get away from there.

In Palm City we were fortunate to find a real doctor who dug the lead out of Reuben's leg and cleaned up his wounds. My man was pretty shaken up about the whole thing, especially the proximity of the shotgun pellets to his groin. I suggested stopping at a tourist court to rest up from our traumas, but he insisted that we drive all the way home to Sarasota, "even if it takes us all night."

Killing Bacon, the first time Reuben had shot anyone to death, evidently shook him up, too, because when we got back to his house he handed me his badge.

"I just had enough of this," he said. At the time I let it go. We were both too tired to argue.

Reuben did leave law enforcement and returned to agriculture, which was fine with me because I had plenty of work needing to be done in the groves of my farm. Sadly, Deputy Reuben Ephram got very little public acclaim for putting down a villain whose most notorious killing had happened more than twenty years before. Nobody had liked Ed Bacon then, and nobody cared about his demise now. At least, I hoped so. I didn't need to be dodging ghosts from our pioneer days.

CHAPTER FIVE

THE SCOTS COME TO SARASOTA

I held onto the City Marshal job for about four more years, until right after the Great War. At the end, a more professional group of bootleggers and whiskey-runners moved in, and I got tired of chasing them around and sometimes getting shot at. That was not the retirement plan I wanted.

It was Clarinda made me quit, but I was ready to. Our little homestead was doing well, and we'd bought two other tracts giving us more than 100 acres. We had most of that in oranges, an operation Reuben helped me run with some hired men, including one of the Ephram sons, and then an Ephram grandson. We felt that I should just live out the rest of my time raising fruit, a job that ain't so dangerous as arguing with purveyors of illegal alcohol.

And that brings us closer to the present.

But wait, I forgot to mention the Scots.

They were the victims of the first really big land swindle around here, the first of many, and it took a fellow Scotsman to do it. This happened in the early days of our community, back when Sarasota was still a tiny speck on the map.

They said that the Gillespies were Scottish lords. What I know is that they owned the Florida Mortgage and Investment Company, which acquired about 50,000 acres of real estate in the county. This was not long after our postmaster had been murdered by the Assassination Society, and these Gillespies picked up some of his land plus big tracts of trees and saw palmettos where wild cattle foraged, which was mostly what there was around here in those days.

The first thing the Gillespies did was to peddle a big chunk of their holdings to their fellow Scottish countrymen with the promise that Sarasota was a land of balmy weather, sunny beaches and fertile soil, all of which was true, but they left out the fact that there were no roads, hotels, or even a town really. But the Scots were promised nice houses waiting for them, ready to move into, which they could buy on time, and that in a few years their tracts would be worth millions. All of these folks, more than twenty families of them, paid their 100 pounds sterling for their starter homes and 40-acre pieces of paradise, all sight unseen.

We townspeople didn't know about this until the Scotsmen suddenly showed up. A side-wheel steamship appeared in the Bay and put them all ashore in the middle of winter at a little wharf that had been thrown together by the beach. I wasn't there, but it must have been quite a sight: men, women and children wandering about putting up tents for shelter. Having been assured that there would be new houses awaiting them, they were surprised to find that there was nothing for them to move into. The company's agent, one Selvin Tate, who claimed to be the nephew of the Archbishop of Canterbury, assured them that the lumber had all been ordered, but that the shipment had been delayed. It quickly became obvious to the Scots that they were on their own. Some of the prominent local families, the Abbes and the Whitakers, the Crocker's and the Tatums, saw their plight and took the women and children into their homes. They took the stronger souls out fishing for mullet. The men had enough success to have a big New Year's Day fish fry and feast and experience the best welcome to Florida that the neighborhood could provide.

The news soon got to me, and I arrived at their campground in time to hear this man Selvin Tate lead a prayer service. He read a passage from the Bible to the effect that, "All we, like poor sheep, have gone astray." These words were met with audible grumbling and groans, so Tate quickly turned the program over to his local "land manager," who happened to be Jasper Braxton. This was a local big-shot who I knew was personally responsible for burning out squatters on any property he wanted to own. He was rich and getting richer.

Braxton showed them the blueprints for their fabulous "Ormiston Colony" but couldn't guaranty when construction would actually begin. He did take the grownups, in shifts by horse and buggy, out to see the properties they now owned. I watched them heading off down the road toward their proposed little community on what is now Fruitville Road, and I saw a day-long parade of proud and angry people. The land they were being taken to was all scrub and range for wild cattle. I don't know exactly what was said or what was done, but I do know that

Selvin Tate fled from Sarasota that night never to be seen again. Over the next several days a few of the Scots, having little in the way of food but maybe a few friends somewhere in America, also abandoned their dream and left for parts unknown.

Some of the tougher ones, perhaps possessed of a bit of money, tried to settle down and make a go of farming, which as you may understand requires clearing land, acquiring livestock, obtaining good tools, and having the ability to use them. So it was a rough go for these settlers. I know because I rode out to see what was happening and encountered a colonist named John Lawrie in his woodland "paradise." He filled me in on how this had come to pass for him and his friends and how they'd all been cheated of their life's savings. He was anxious for paying work, which there wasn't much of at the time, and we discussed how he might cut and sell a stand of his timber. I ended up doing some work for him, bringing my saws and horse and helping him take down some tall pine trees, for a share of what they would bring at the mill. I don't recall if I ever collected that money because a freeze set in and wiped out whatever resolve these pioneers might still have had to conquer Florida. Almost all of them broke camp and headed north.

What I did get out of my conversations with John Lawrie was a better understanding of who Robert Burns was.

As I've said, Captain MacFarlane, accepted to be my dad, died when I was four. He bequeathed me a little book of Burns' songs which I'm told my father carried along with him when he was fighting for the Confederacy in John Tyler Morgan's Alabama Cavalry. There were a lot of words in these songs, poems to me, that I didn't know the meaning of or how you said them, like "bleerit knurl," "braw wooer," and "craps and kye," and Lawrie laughed and explained them. He helped me understand a little bit about my MacFarlane ancestors, though what he knew about my recent family wasn't much. Lawrie believed that the old time MacFarlanes were from the county Lennox and, hundreds and hundreds of years ago, had fought "with swords huge enough to require two hands" against the army of Mary Queen of Scots. They proved themselves to be "valiant light footmen," he told me. But John Lawrie didn't know one single thing about the accomplishments of any MacFarlanes in the centuries since that battle. He thought they might have moved to Ireland.

I found it strange that anyone would remember a name or a battle from that far back and yet not have a shred of information about the intervening years. Lawrie further explained, with his cheeks glowing, that an ancient Scotsman named Wallace, which was my father's given name, was a fearless, estimable, admirable, and altogether excellent Scottish hero.

To me, these poor Scots marooned in Sarasota were not just victims of a cruel fraud but were also heroes - for having the gumption to sail an ocean and come to a country none had ever seen, all to reach a remote tropical wilderness such as Florida was back then. They paid heavily for their courage, but that seemed to be something of a tradition in Scotland.

The scheme damaged them but, unfortunately, did not hurt the schemers any. One of these charming Gillespies showed up from Scotland to manage the family empire in Sarasota while all of this was going on. Despite his encouraging words, the Scottish colony broke up. But Gillespie carried on to build the big DeSoto Hotel downtown, and the city wharf, and he cleared our Main Street as a way to get to that hotel. He built a big house to live in and a nine-hole golf course, the first one in Florida. And he got elected as our first mayor as soon as the town incorporated. I had to work for him, as City Marshal. And guess who ended up owning those 40-acre lots the Scotsmen paid for? Jasper Braxton, of course. And eventually that real estate actually did pay off. Braxton made lots of money, selling the lots to the Yankees who started pouring in. He got so rich he couldn't pay attention to his wife.

CHAPTER SIX

BERTHA PALMER
CHANGED OUR LIVES

After the Scots, after the Ashley Gang, and after the shootouts with Charley Willard, Dr. Andrews and Ed Bacon, I retired as City Marshal. I'd had enough. And I stayed retired from anything related to enforcing the law for almost five years.

In 1918 the Great War ended, and my son Mack came home. He had volunteered for the Army as soon as he turned eighteen, but he didn't make it to France. He only got shipped as far as England before peace was declared. I sent him a letter suggesting he try to visit the "family homestead" in Scotland, but he never got to it. I don't suppose they were giving those boys any time off to traipse around the countryside anyway.

Other than being worried about Mack's welfare, and the ladies all being busy knitting sweaters for the troops, that war didn't seem to affect us much in Sarasota. Of course, the Coast Guard's big cutter Tampa, which led the Gasparilla Festival every year in February, was called into action and sailed away. She ended up being torpedoed, as I understand it, off the coast of Wales. That's a long ways from home. They calculate that it was the biggest naval disaster of that terrible war, with 126 Coast Guardsmen and sailors lost. A lot of them were our boys from around here.

About the time the soldiers were coming home, Mrs. Bertha Palmer died in Osprey.

That was big news because this lady and her two sons had, in just a few years, bought up about a third of Manatee County. A hundred thousand acres at least. Maybe two hundred thousand. Nobody that rich, not even the Gillespies, had ever been imagined around here before. And on that vast swath of land she started putting up barns and pens and raising cattle. Not just capturing wild livestock wherever you happened upon them out on the range, which was the practice when I was a young boy, but introducing prize animals. She dipped them for ticks, which none of the other cattlemen thought necessary. And she built fences that ran for miles.

She built mansions, too. The biggest was in Osprey, which until then had just been a few fishermen and a lot of mangroves. I got to see that place once soon after she died, and I just can't describe it other than to say it was the most beautiful park, the most beautiful country house, the shadiest pathways, the prettiest lawns and fountains, you could ever picture. She brought in rich northerners in the wintertime to party at that house and soak up the sun and to fish for trophies to hang on their walls. She was the sun, and made the whole of Sarasota Bay the place to be if you were a Vanderbilt or a Carnegie or a Field, or whoever else was rolling in too much money to count.

With her sudden passing, the whole Palmer empire was inherited by her two boys, Honoré and Potter. They immediately went to work turning everything they had inherited into dollar bills. It was them, Honoré mostly, who opened up the big celery fields farm out on Fruitville. It grew to employ hundreds of poor, but industrious, folk, working in the muck and growing the finest, biggest celery you ever did see. I'm here to say, this happened in almost no time at all. That's what a big bank account can do. They sold any land they didn't have any immediate use for to smaller real estate developers, who then kicked out any squatters and hermits who hadn't already been run off. The Palmers leased out miles of pine woods to turpentine tappers and lumber mills. And they began handing out jobs. This is how, after several years of being a farmer – we called ourselves growers - I got back into the law enforcement business.

I was respected in Sarasota due to my reputation as an honest lawman, which was known to be a rarity. I also had a good business producing fruit and shipping it north. The big boys even talked to me about running for City Council or the Statehouse. I laughed and said no, as politely as I could. Politics is for crooks. The only honest politician I ever met was Captain Duff, and he only lasted one term as County Sheriff. I didn't need any political favors and didn't plan to start selling them either.

The Palmers knew about me because their land ran around the back of mine, and we'd never had any disagreement about where the line was. I'd had my farm surveyed by Charles Johnson, who later got the job as County Surveyor, so his name on my plat stood me in good stead when the Palmers' land man first showed up. His name was Kelsey.

He was a tall man, black-haired and clean shaven and wearing quality work clothes that looked to have been pressed and starched that morning, and he came in from the back of the property, through the woods, on a horse. Most everybody else connected with the Palmers had started driving cars. This man had a cut-off varmint-blaster in a case hung on his saddle and looked like a spiffed-up version of all the old-time cowboys I had ever known.

This was probably in September, a couple of months after Mrs. Palmer died, and he caught me sitting outside my warehouse counting empty orange crates and figuring out how many new ones I'd need to get Joe Kroft to make for me at his shop over in Bee Ridge.

He addressed me as Mr. MacFarlane and asked if I might spare a moment to talk.

"About what?" I asked.

He introduced himself as a Palmer man and wondered if I agreed that the big pine tree beside the Cowhorn Spring was where my property line began.

"That's right," I said. "It corners there."

"That's what I thought," he said, and looked uncomfortable talking down from the saddle.

"Well, come on in," I invited and walked into my office. He got off his horse, tied it to the corral gate and followed me in. Turned out that when he stood on the ground he wasn't as tall as me, but he did outweigh me. "Kelsey's my name," he said, and I offered him a chair, the only one there was except the one at my own desk, which I had made myself one long winter out of some blackjack branches I'd picked up on my travels. Kelsey had brought maps.

After settling on his seat and taking in the atmosphere of place, which was a drafty old barn full of my wood crates and farming implements, he explained what he did.

"I'm a land man and general manager for the Palmer family farms, which I'll call the Sarasota-Venice Company …"

"What do they call it?" I interrupted.

He tilted his head to one side. He could do that and his eyes never left yours. "Well, they'll be calling it the Palmer Farms and Experimental Station, but it's all the same." I was impressed with the name and what it suggested for the future, so I smiled and asked him if he'd like any grapefruit juice to drink. He declined.

From his leather tube, he peeled away a single map and pulled it out. I could see that it was just one of the many he had in there. He spread it out on my desk, and we held it in place with a couple of my mementoes: my first deputy's badge that I unpinned from Captain Duff's shirt after he was shot in the chest by that degenerate Charley Willard; another was the book of verse by Robert Burns that had seen me through many a lonely night.

Kelsey seemed to ignore those important and informative objects and ran his fingers over the plat. He pointed out my land and then a whole lot of other people's parcels that I knew had all sold out years ago to the Palmers.

"Now this is where we think you own," he said, tapping his finger at a spot about where we were sitting. I took a full minute to study his chart. I got up and walked around to look over his shoulder to see it from all sides. I could smell the Boraxo in his shirt. I traced the line down to McIntosh Road where it was supposed to go, then east to where it crossed the creek and went about six hundred yards more, then north, making my back line.

"Seems about right," I said. In fact, it looked like he might have given me an extra twenty feet or so along the back. "But you know, I have other property south of here and some lots in Sarasota, Venice and Englewood."

"Yes sir," Kelsey acknowledged, rolling up his map. "I saw references down at the courthouse, but those pieces don't concern me. They don't butt up to any of our land." With that he got up and stuffed the map back in his case.

"Are you looking to buy me out?" I asked. If he was, we were headed in a bad direction.

"Nope, Mr. MacFarlane. We've got all the land we need. I'm just verifying that you and our other neighbors out this way are amicable about what belongs to you and what belongs to us."

"That's fine, then. I'd say your map has got it straight."

We shook hands, and he mounted up. "I understand that you used to be a lawman," he said from the saddle.

"I was, for quite a few years," I admitted.

"I've heard some stories," he said, "You brought a few bad men to justice."

"I'm glad that's what people say about me." Actually I had brought down more than a few bad men, but I thought to mention it would sound like I was bragging.

"I was once in the law business myself," he said. "Up in Illinois." He kicked his horse and rode away.

I didn't think much more about it, though naturally I was curious, everybody was, to see how the Palmer land holdings were to be developed. Their property was just so huge that however it was changed couldn't help shaping and molding our lives in the years to come.

I told Clarinda about my visitor when I went in for supper. She cooked with wood back then on a Wedgewood stove. They had brought some electricity to town, but it was only to run an ice plant for the fishermen. It would be several years before it got out to us.

She laughed and said, "They sure did know who you are and what you'd like. The way he showed up on a horse."

That made me blush and deny it. Yet Clarinda was delighted to hear any tidbits of news about the Palmer family. For the preceding eight years the favorite item of gossip around here had been anything to do with Mrs. Palmer. Her passing away had knocked a big hole in everybody's conversational topics. It even dried up the minister's sermons at our church, since he loved to preach about the contrast between good works and money, riding to heaven on faith, not gold, whether or not God rewards the righteous with earthly goods, the sins of avarice and greed, and so forth.

"What did he say they were going to do with all those woods behind us?" Clarinda wanted to know.

"That didn't come up," I explained. "We didn't get that well acquainted."

"My lands," she exclaimed. "Seems like you could have found out something. I've got to believe this will be progress for us. And probably sooner than we think."

She was right about sooner than I thought, though I'm not sure it was progress. About one week later, Kelsey rode back up and offered me a job. There was a need, he said, for a local man in their security department, which was headed up by a man from Chicago. He mentioned that they also had a contract for "certain services" with the Southern Detective Bureau. I didn't say it, but I knew these "detectives" to be gun thugs used mostly to throw people out of their houses or deal harshly with anybody ever believed to have mouthed the words: "labor union." Kelsey must have seen something in my face because he asked if I had a problem with that.

"I don't like their methods," I told him.

He shrugged. "I don't either," he said. "But you probably won't ever have to deal with them. I'm just giving you the big picture about how we view our public safety set-up. Your job would be to keep the peace, run off trespassers, deal with petty thieves and wife-beaters among our employees, keep alcohol out, regular police work."

"What about the sheriff?" At that time our County Sheriff was L.G. Wingate, a man for whom I had little respect, and our City Marshal was Bixby Hodges, for whom I had even less. (The reason for my lack of respect was that the way most lawmen had started to make money was to put a lot of people, colored people mostly, in jail and then send them out on chain gangs to clear private roads, or else lease them to the timber companies and to big farmers who appreciated cheap labor and could work the men like slaves.)

"The sheriff's men don't come on Palmer property unless we ask for them, which we never have," Kelsey said. "If someone were to steal one of our tractors or turbine pumps and run off to Bradenton with it, we'd work with the sheriff, sure, and he'd work with us."

"It's unlikely Sheriff Wingate would contribute much as far as getting your property back," I had to say.

"That's where you would come in. Along with the head of our Public Safety Department, Burna Levi."

"The one they call 'Heinie'?"

"That's him. You know him?"

"I've never met him. I just heard his name as someone who works for the Palmers. With that name, is he some kind of a German?"

"He may in fact be. Why don't you ask him yourself? Come over to the office tomorrow and we can all talk."

"Where would that be? In the Bank of Sarasota Building?" I knew that was where Palmer headquarters was.

"Not that office. The farm office off of Fruitville." I knew where that was, too.

The work sounded easy enough, and it could be interesting – getting to know the Palmer operation from the inside. We made arrangements for the next day, but I told him I needed to talk to my wife about the idea of me taking a job again. That didn't impress him much, but he said he hoped I could make it and left. I was torn, in a way. I had a similar offer made to me once before. By Jasper Braxton. That's a story with a sad ending that makes me smile.

But you don't get offered a paying position every day, especially not one with the biggest landowner in Florida, and I was still, by my reckoning, in considerably better shape than the average man of 50. So I was pretty sure I was going to be there for the meeting.

When I told Clarinda about it that afternoon she was more excited than I was. It seems she thought it wouldn't be such a bad idea if I was to get off the place more, you know, keep an eye on all the goings-on in the world. In other words, get out from underfoot. Beginning with her own dad, Pa Barlow, Clarinda had little patience with a man hanging around the home place during working hours. But she didn't actually say that. She did reveal, however, that she had some ideas about how to spend the extra money this might bring in, like getting a new car to replace the old Tin Lizzie we bought the year before Mack had to go into the Army, before we knew there would be a war. Clarinda had taught herself to drive, watching me, and was apt to ride off on her lonesome to church or to her women's meetings, or to wherever she took a notion to go. If I wasn't around to do it, she got pretty good at cranking that old car by herself.

CLARINDA BARLOW MACFARLANE'S STORY

There was a time when Gawain and I as were close to each other as two peas in a pod. Isn't that the way the Bible reads? Cleave only unto each other? We cleaved and made it work, our lives and our little farm, the two of us and our baby. Those were my happiest years, when Wallace was a wee mite. Gawain — they started calling him Gabe because it was more familiar to the ear — had his job and prominence in our community. He was proud to wear a badge, and I was proud that he was my husband.

He never liked his employers very much, or anyone else he thought had too much authority, and that's the way I was raised too. To hell with those who don't do for themselves but live off the sweat of others. To hell with them! That's not a Christian thing to say, but it's the way I feel. Gawain thinks they're all hypocrites, and he means all the politicians, all of his bosses, all the real estate developers. I'd laugh and say, "Who do you like?" "Just regular people," he'd say. "And special ones, like you."

I've thought about that some. The "regular people" covers quite a lot of the crowd. I can't say I care for all of them myself. But Gawain and I have been solid in our community here between the creeks. We've made our way, and I have friends. The church is a great support.

Everyone has times when they feel lonely. I have quiet nights when Gawain tries to break through to me. But it's no use. I'm stuck somewhere back in the woods twenty years ago, dreaming and hoping for something better. And knowing it's never going to come.

"You've just got the blues, honey," he'll say.

Like the blues was a headache that would soon go away. A lot of times, though, it's my life.

On good days, I realize that the "something better" I've yearned for is actually what I have, settled here with Gawain. But when he's not off working he's holed up in his office reading some farmer magazine. Our son Wallace, or Mack as we call him, has left for the Army. I get very lonely by myself. There's always something that needs doing around the house or the farm, but we never have much fun. I was raised poor, and many a night I went to bed hungry, so maybe I wouldn't even know fun if I saw it.

Gawain and I never go anywhere. The seasons never change here. And here I go complaining again. Maybe I just think too hard about things. Listen to me – going on about nothing.

CHAPTER SEVEN
PALMER FARMS

The gravel road east from Sarasota to Fruitville and on to the Myakka was straight as an arrow and well-travelled by car and mule-drawn wagon. A sign for Palmer Farms told you where to turn off, which was onto another straight gravel road headed due south to arrive at an orderly cluster of white one-story buildings. The simple one marked "Office" was concrete, solid and square – like something the school board or government might build. It was a lot more substantial than most of the stores and houses in our area. Through the glass doors I found a counter, and two women behind it busily pecking away at their typewriters. One of them with white hair, older than me I hoped, looked up and said, "If your name is Gabe MacFarlane you're expected."

I smiled and said that's who I was. She announced in a loud voice, "Mister Levi! He's here!"

Mister Levi appeared from the back, and beckoned me to come around the counter. He was a square man, not very tall, and had the fringes of a beard outlining his jaw. He was wearing a white shirt with a black tie, and he gave my hand a workout when he shook it and told me to come on in.

His was the first office we came to. I learned later that there were four offices in all: one belonging to Honoré Palmer and the others were assigned to the land manager I'd met, Kelsey, a "procurement director" whose name I didn't get, and of course Mr. Levi, who was in charge of police business.

"I run security for the family," is how Burna Levi put it. He explained what my job would be. It was much as Kelsey had described it: get on the ground, keep out liquor, prevent thefts, investigate crimes, and handle the disorderly. At the moment, the Palmers had only about twenty people working on the project, which was to drain an 8,000-acre section of wet marshy muck and make it ready to farm. But within the month he anticipated another fifty men would be hired. In time, when crops could be planted, there would be hundreds more, at least seasonally. And more acres would be drained. The crop was going to be celery.

There were other "projects" as well, including ones further to the east, involving cattle raising and timber management, on an enormous tract that ran all the way to Myakka Lake. And another project laying south across Phillippi Creek which was being leased out for turpentine tapping. Burna would like me to make my presence known at all of these locations, though all were well-managed and trouble was rare. When I did happen to be at the Fruitville Road office, I was welcome to take a desk out front "with the girls," or I could find space out in the equipment shed. That was the big barn across the gravel road from the office.

He went by either Burna or "Heinie," he said. The latter name he'd picked up in the recent Great War in which he had served as a translator, interviewing German prisoners in France, because he spoke their language. Where he got that, apparently, was growing up in Chicago in a family of beer makers. He had no background whatsoever in police work, and he expected to leave any "riding the range," or "rough stuff," as he put it, in my hands. We discussed my salary, which I found quite satisfactory.

"I have this job," Heinie said, smiling thinly through his whiskers, "because the Palmer family found that I was honest with money. Over time, I've earned their trust. Mr. Kelsey said that you have a reputation as an honest man, too, and I hope you will prove to be just that." I wasn't sure whether I was supposed to feel complimented or warned by this welcome, but I just replied that I was ready to start proving. He said to come back in the morning about eight o'clock, and he'd have one of the engineers give me a tour of the place. Heinie, however, wouldn't be there. Rather he'd be at his city office, in the Sarasota Bank Building where the Palmers managed all of their far-flung enterprises and counted their money. As for visiting the other locations, he showed me a map in the hallway covering all of the Palmer holdings from Osprey to "old" Myakka City, and where I could find a drawer full of even more maps. Seeing all these maps is what really made me want to take the job. I'd ridden over much of this land without really knowing where I was, and it was fascinating to me to see the landscape, the creeks, the coastline, the river banks and especially the property lines – who owned what - all laid out for my study.

One other thing, Burna reminded me in parting. "The current

Sarasota City Marshal and the current sheriff, and all of their deputies, have limited jurisdiction here." I liked the sound of that.

But he added that by the same token, the Palmers asserted limited jurisdiction over the turpentine and logging camps on their properties. These were under leases to other companies. Those camps, I knew, housed a few white wage workers but mainly they employed convict labor. Black workers comprised the bulk of that workforce. All of them lived within stockades. The only difference was that the convicts didn't have to pay for their food and lodging while the white wage workers did, but their bill for the hospitality just about equaled their so-called wages. All involved were the poorest of the poor. The camps had their own "law enforcement."

CLARINDA BARLOW MACFARLANE'S STORY (continued)

 I was enthusiastic that Gawain got that job. It would keep him out of the house and reading farm journals half the day. I liked the part about the money, and I was serious about getting a new car, one with a push-button starter. The old Ford we owned leaked oil and overheated regularly and was definitely unreliable.

It had occurred to me that I might start a business of my own. For fun I had been wrapping up gift baskets, full of fruit and sea-grape jelly and orange-juice candy, to sell to tourists at our country store. That could be a business. Or maybe I'd think of some place to go, and just go there.

Palmer Farms sounded like a safe place to me. It seemed unlikely that Gawain would get himself hurt or killed, like he easily might have done subduing drunks and outlaws in Sarasota, and he wouldn't just get fat and lazy like an old farmer. I could see sunnier days to come.

I reported as scheduled and found the chief engineer, Ormond Ludlow, in the big equipment barn. He was a ruddy, round-faced man with yellow hair and a yellow beard, and he used red suspenders to hold up his pants. Sitting behind his desk covered with papers, he frowned to see me come through the door.

"MacFarlane?" he asked, taking off his delicate gold-rimmed spectacles.

"That's me. And you are?"

"Ludlow," he introduced himself. "Chief Project Engineer. I'm to drive you around so you can see the operation we've undertaken. Not that most people understand drainage," he added.

"Water runs downhill?" I suggested.

That got a little smile. "That's the gist of it," he said, softening a bit. "Let's be off."

He had a nice International Harvester truck, better than I'd ever ridden in though I'd seen them around. It had a funny sloped hood and a wooden frame around the bed. He must have sensed my appreciation because he said, "Model F," proudly.

It started up smooth as could be, and we were off, trailing a cloud of dust.

What we saw were mechanical excavators as big as locomotives riding on tank treads, shoveling yards of dirt into red Mack trucks. The trucks hauled their loads out to the edges of the marshy meadowlands and dumped them upon already tall piles. Those piles of soil where to be spread over other sections of land. Some of the spreading was done by machine – I saw one bulldozer – but a lot of it was done by a squad of laborers with rakes and shovels. I saw coffer dams blocking the natural streams into gurgling ponds. And pipes were being laid to carry the runoff water southward, to some place far, far away.

It was the grandest land and water moving project I had ever seen or imagined. The point of it was to convert thousands of fertile but soggy acres, prone to seasonal overflow, into prime agricultural land.

All of the unnecessary water, I suspected, was being channeled in the general direction of either Phillippi Creek or Catfish Creek, down which it would flow into Little Sarasota Bay. My own farm was downstream, beside Catfish Creek, and it had flooded once in the past twenty years, so I started wondering about the wisdom of this. But I didn't say anything about it.

Just as interesting to me was the primer Ormond Ludlow gave me as we rode along - about the Palmers' overall plans. I was all ears to hear about them and his complaints about the celery fields being just one of the many big ideas the family had. There was also the cattle ranching on land steadily being fenced in at what they called Meadowsweet Pastures by the Myakka River, and Ludlow wasn't happy that he wasn't being involved in that at all. Then there was the leased land, the turpentine and logging camps, and he just rolled his eyes when he mentioned those projects.

"Leasing the properties for logging is just a way the Palmers get someone else to do the work for them," he complained. "First the trees are tapped out of the turpentine, then they're cut down for lumber. Then the land is cleared. And once you do that, why you can sell house lots! And Gabe," we were on a first-name basis now, "that's the heart of it all! You know as well as I do that anything around here that can be broken up into little lots is selling like hotcakes. Like hotcakes!"

He was right about that. There were more real estate agents than there were farmers in Sarasota. And more lots were for sale than there was dry land to build houses on.

"And you," Ludlow exclaimed excitedly, pointing his pen right at my nose. "You are a very important part of this now!"

The job settled into a pattern. I'd ride out to Palmer Farms early in the morning and spend most of the day riding around in my company truck, or a horse if I wanted, and getting to know the staff and telling them they could call me if there was any trouble. I had the use of a Palmer pickup truck, a clunky Ford that had been converted from a passenger car, and this saved a lot of wear and tear on my own junker. On most days I could take time to park in the shade of a tree and sip from a thermos of coffee while reading a newspaper or book. I got interested in the *Lone Wolf* by Louis Joseph Vance. I was supposed to keep sheets recording my time, but nobody ever looked at them. Since there wasn't any trouble, I stopped turning them in.

On Fridays and Saturdays my routine was a little different. I'd sleep late with Clarinda at my house and not get to work till around lunchtime. That way I could stay on the job until midnight, just poking around, making the rounds to be sure there wasn't any weekend wickedness going on. Clarinda packed me a lunchbox, and I usually ate out in the equipment shed. That's how I got to know Otto, a mechanic from Rhode Island who hadn't worked for the Palmers much longer than I had. He was a friendly fellow, but his face was off center. His jaw sloped to the right since he only had half a mouthful of teeth.

"Damn trailer hitch popped loose, flew up and knocked 'em out. Knocked me out, too."

He had a good attitude about it. Said the distortion made it easier to clamp down on his cigar, which he was always chewing on, lit or unlit, unless he was taking food. He lived in a room above a hardware store in Bee Ridge and was courting a girl who was a waitress. He said he loved Florida because there was no snow. I had to admit that I had never laid my eyes on the stuff except in picture books.

I took advantage of Burna Levi's offer and drove out to see the other Palmer enterprises, starting with Meadowsweet Pastures. I called ahead and got to meet with the farm manager at his office. He offered me a horse, and we rode out to the pens where the hands were dipping cows in an arsenic solution to kill off the ticks. This was a controversial innovation but only because our local ranchers hadn't ever done it. The practice caught on when it turned out to make Florida beef more marketable. And we rode out to where his crew had constructed a bridge across the Myakka River. From the middle of that bridge you could see miles of sun-speckled marshland, oak hammocks, and open pastures dotted with some of the fattest cows ever bred in Florida.

The farm's manager said they hadn't had any crime in three years, nor any disruptions except a couple of fistfights to settle personal matters, but he'd remember to call me right away in the event of any infractions. "The Palmers want everything kept peaceful, and if I have any problem I can't handle you'll hear about it pronto," he assured me. It was a very enjoyable day.

I recall that the first Friday night I spent there, driving around the Farms after dark, with all the work stopped and the employees gone home, was just as peaceful and pleasant as it would have been on my own front porch after our evening meal, with me and Clarinda watching the moon come up. In some ways it was even better, since I was getting paid to enjoy the miles-wide vistas and the earth-scented fresh air, without a single light to mar the sight except the headlamps of the occasional car passing on Fruitville Road. It was almost like when I rode the trail in the old days, before all the people came. I thought about building a campfire and heating up a pot of coffee on the embers, but instead I went into the equipment barn and boiled a cup on our little Sterno stove.

The Farms had what you might call a night watchman. He was a mean old cracker who drank, and he slept most of the night in the little sentry box by the front gate. His name was Flem, and seeing my lantern shining in the equipment barn was enough to entice him to hobble the half mile down the farm road to see if I needed anything. I gave him a cup of coffee, which he took, and he turned his head to take a snort from a dented silver flask, which he did not offer to share with me.

"It is so quiet the only thing I'm scared could sneak up on me would be a black widow spider," he said.

"See many of them around here?" I asked, checking around my feet.

"Sure, I do. No telling what else is creeping around in that little shack of mine. I keep that lantern going full blast, but sometimes it burns all the air out of the room, and I have to step outside. I can't see a damn thing when I do," he complained. "If some bastard wanted to catch me unawares, right then would be the time to do it. They could split my skull wide open before I knew what hit me. Got any chew?"

"I don't do it," I told him. "I don't drink on the job, either."

"Didn't say you did," he insisted. "You'd get fired for that." I realized he believed his flask was invisible.

I didn't care whether he drank or not. I just wished he'd been better company.

While I was out of the house working, Clarinda spent her time becoming involved in politics. First it was the Anti-Saloon League which was pretty popular in our church and the other congregations in our neighborhood. I asked her why this interested her, and she said it was because her father had been a heavy drinker in need of instruction and temperance. Personally I had always thought Mr. Barlow was too poor to afford becoming a drunk and too hungry to do much besides work all day tending to his garden and his bony livestock, but whatever Clarinda wanted to say was okay. After all it was her father.

On the subject of drinking, Clarinda had never objected that I enjoyed a whiskey or two with Reuben when he dropped over in the evening, or when my son needed some advice or wanted to give me some. And she liked a glass of sherry herself, or a sip of brandy on special occasions. But I was glad to see her spreading her wings and joining a group that included some of the younger wives and mothers. The League was also pushing for women's right to vote, and I was all for that. The good ol' boys had screwed up everything they could, and stolen whatever they wanted no matter who got killed, for as long as I'd known anything about politics. Giving women the right to vote might help change some of that. It sure couldn't make it any worse.

Clarinda also kept bringing up that new car, and before too many weeks had passed we drove down to the automobile dealership in Osprey and traded in for an almost-new 1920 Dodge Brothers touring car with a buggy top. The big selling point for Clarinda was the starter button on the floor. I signed the note, but she got to drive us home. I'd never seen her any happier.

THE MURDER OF PA BARLOW

 It didn't take much to get Pa Barlow drunk.

So far out in the country, the arrival of a roaming cowboy was a surprise and welcome company for an evening's companionship, especially when the stranger offered to fry up a skillet of pork chops and onions and produced a bottle of whiskey.

The man said he'd prefer to camp outside. In truth, Pa Barlow's cabin near Horse Creek wasn't much for comfort. Outside was better, and the boundless bright lights of the Milky Way floating high above the rim of cabbage palms and tall pines were so beautiful that a man wanted to think about God and eternity.

Add a campfire and the stranger's guitar, and Pa could forget the day's struggles with all the troublesome weeds in his sweet potato patch and with his loneliness – though there was a woman inside.

He was aroused from his reverie when the stranger offered him a paper to sign. "None of that for me," Pa said, alerted to danger. "I don't sign anything!"

"This is nothing," the man said, "It recognizes your rights and pays you..."

"To hell with that," Pa muttered and fell asleep.

Did he wake up when the wagon rolled over him?

The stranger pulled the wagon a ways down the road and waited. Later, the woman inside found Pa, cold and stiff, and she ran away into the woods where cicadas roared. The stranger followed her there and took her away.

Days passed before a neighbor from afar passed by and found the corpse, lying beside the cabin burned beyond repair. Whether it was because the campfire spread and consumed the house or a lightning strike took it, who knows? Or maybe the stranger decided things would be better with the house gone.

The neighbor buried Pa in the soft tilled earth of the potato patch and planted a cross of tree limbs tied together.

He discovered that there was a horse and cow in the stable, one pained with milk and both spent with hunger. The neighbor herded them through the prairie to his homestead miles away.

Our first trip in that new car was a sad one. Clarinda mailed her dad a birthday card - right before the war we got pretty good rural free delivery in Manatee County – and it came back "Occupant Moved." Well, we knew that was wrong. Pa was in his 70s, and whatever else might have happened to him he certainly wasn't going to move off his farm without letting anybody know.

What used to be a two or three-day wagon ride was now about a six hour drive, unless the car got stuck on a muddy road, blew a tire or busted an axle. Clarinda was hell-bent to figure out about her Pa. We loaded up the car and headed that way the same day her dad's birthday card got returned to us.

The Barlow homestead was still far back in the country. Pulling into the driveway, however, was the end of all that was familiar. The house had burned to the ground and vines had begun to cover the remains. The barn roof had collapsed as if in sympathy. Clarinda stared out the window in shock. Then she bolted from the car and went racing about the place yelling for her father. She flushed a nest of mocking birds from a shrub by the ruins and a black snake from the stones that had held up the porch.

When Clarinda calmed down we walked around. There was plenty of nature, but no sign of human life. Given the healthy layer of weeds about the place I guessed that the fire had occurred at least two months prior to our visit. There was nothing in the charred pile of building debris that was worth salvaging. Anything of value had likely been picked over by someone before us. Clarinda found something though, a blue tin mug with half of the enamel chipped off, leaving some rusty spots. She carried it along with her as we walked and took it back to the car when we decided to leave.

We drove down the dirt road about two miles and came upon a neighbor's house. There was a man sitting on the porch, and once he understood our business he offered to go back with us and show us where he had buried Pa. His name was Tibbs.

"He'd been dead a few days when I found him. I couldn't tell much about the cause of death because, you know..."

"But he wasn't burned up?" Clarinda asked.

"No," Tibbs said flatly. "Didn't appear to be shot, either. Could have had a heart attack."

He took us to spot in the garden where he had buried Pa, and we both stepped away so that Clarinda could pray by herself. She sat down on the ground and mouthed some words softly.

"What's going to happen to this place now?" Tibbs inquired.

"I don't know," I told him. "It'll be up to her."

"They'll take it for taxes if you don't watch out."

"I don't even know what county we're in," I admitted.

"It's been DeSoto, but now they say it might be Charlotte next year. So I don't know what to tell you. But if you want to sell it . . ." his voice trailed off.

"Like I said, it'll be up to her."

Clarinda rejoined us. "That was mighty kind of you to get Pa in the ground," she said to Tibbs. "I reckon we ought to get you home."

We crammed into the car and drove back the way we'd come.

"I ain't going to sell the farm," Clarinda said from the back seat. "I've got too many memories here."

After waving goodbye to Tibbs and his lonely house we decided to extend our trip by driving to Arcadia, and we got to the courthouse about twenty minutes before the clerk's office closed. Fortunately, we were in the right county, and it didn't take the helpful lady long to find the Barlow place in her records. She knew her county a lot better than we did.

She spread out a big book on the counter top. "There has been a lot of activity in that area," she explained. "Ah, here it is. Now, it looks like no taxes are owed because they've been paid up by a 'Horse Creek

Ranch, Inc.'"

"That ain't right!" Clarinda slammed her hand down on the counter, and the clerk jumped back.

"I'm afraid that is the situation," she said. "There were three years of taxes due, and this Horse Creek ranch has paid them. If no one redeems the property it will go for judgment to Horse Creek in two more years."

"I'm going to fight this," Clarinda warned the woman.

"Now wait a second," I broke in, trying to calm things down. "What's this about redeeming, and how much would it cost?"

"I can figure that up for you," the clerk said, and she did her calculations.

She came up with a price, along with penalties and interest, and it was so cheap I could hardly believe it. I could handle it with what was in my wallet.

So, the property was redeemed. Pa was dead, but his little piece of real estate was going to stay in the family. We never did learn any more about how he died. We had our suspicions that somebody was greedy for Pa's land – that was the cause of a lot of murderousness out in the country – but we didn't have any facts to back those suspicions up.

CHAPTER EIGHT

THE TURPENTINE PRISON LABOR CAMP

When we got back from that trip, Clarinda took on the job of finding a lawyer, actually an apprentice lawyer, in Arcadia whose commission was to get the Barlow acres into her name. This gave rise to endless questions, since the claim had never been surveyed or properly titled, and this Horse Creek Ranch, Inc., had a lawyer, too, but she dug into it. Clarinda's way of dealing with life's problems, and now her grief, was to lose herself in work.

I was content to see Clarinda so occupied and left it all in her good hands. My attention went back to my Palmer Ranch job and my desire to see the range of the company's holdings.

I'd seen a map, so I had a pretty good idea where the biggest of the Palmers' turpentine camps was. It took up about 4,000 acres a few miles inland from the coastal town of Venice (which the Palmers owned), in a community the locals called Laurel. It was just east of the new Seaboard Air Line Railway which shot straight through our vast pine forests and scrub prairie, land we thought was without end. Black labor and convict labor laid those tracks, of course. It was quite an impressive achievement.

You could stand on a creosote tie right in the middle of those rails deep in the woods, as I'd done more than once, and as far as the eye could see there was nothing but straight all the way to the blue-sky horizons in either direction. Those tracks ran right past my property.

The big chunk of woods in Laurel where the camp was located was leased by the Palmers to R.S. Hall or George McCloud, I can't recall, but folks referred to it as the McKeithan Still because Sam G. McKeithan ran it.

Being king of the Palmer range, I could take my horse for a long ride when I wanted to. His name was "Pardner," for the obvious reason that he was my pardner. To get to Laurel from my farm on Catfish Creek, it was just about as fast to go on horseback on the old trails beside the Seaboard railroad as it was to drive by road. There was a new highway, but you had to swing all the way out to Nokomis by a gravel road just to get to that highway. On the other hand, I could go on horseback by grassy paths through the woods, right close to the tracks and away from the tourists, back where the farmers lived. Back where I felt at home. Few of those farmers had cars, or tractors either for that matter. By and large they were poor, and many of them knew who I was, and we waved at one another as I rode by.

The McKeithan Still camp had a gate out front instructing me to "Keep Out/Employees Only/Pass Required!"

I was a Palmer employee, which I figured was close enough so I pulled the gate aside and rode on. It wasn't far to another barricade, a barbed wire fence stretched across the road and a sleepy old man with a sweat-stained hat sitting under an umbrella with a pot of lemonade, I guess, on a tree stump beside him. He had a Smith and Wesson repeating rifle on his lap. I didn't have to wake him up. My horse did that by pushing his nose into the guard's face and snorting.

"Ho!" He said with a start and looked up at me. He actually had a badge of some sort pinned to his shirt, which I did not.

"What? Who?" he continued.

"I'm Gabe McFarlane, chief peace officer for the Palmer Farms. Just paying a visit," I said.

"Well, now," he stood up, "We don't take visitors." This fellow had plentiful whiskers and wild blood-shot eyes, but his gun was pointed down and he appeared to be reasonable.

"I'm not paying a social call. I'm under orders to go by all the Palmer properties, just to check. Did you know this was Palmer land?"

"This is McCloud and McKeithan land, I know that."

"The Palmers are in it, too. So let me pass. You can tell me where your boss is."

"Stay here," he told me, and he ran back through the trees, dragging a damaged foot behind him, and carrying his rifle. That left me free to proceed, which I did. Around one sharp turn and there was the stockade, made of ten-foot posts stuck in the ground and each strung with six strands of barbed wire. Behind the fence were a number of long, rough-lumbered buildings, like horse stables without doors. I could only see a few people around in the yard, women who ducked inside leaving a pair of dirty babies crawling about in the sand. One of the grubby tots, happy it seemed, smiled at me. There was also a litter of pigs in the yard. Otherwise, just a blazing hot sun and lizards watching me from the wire.

When the guard came limping back he was followed by a broad-shouldered bald man about my age who had a pistol on his belt. I dismounted.

"Who are you?" he asked, politely enough.

I told him and explained that my mission was just to see the place and how it was run.

"Nobody's ever done that," he objected.

"It's Honoré Palmer," I shrugged. "Just wants me to see your layout and whether you need any back-up."

"Police back-up? No need for that," he assured me, a wide smile on his red face.

"That's fine. So, maybe you could take me around and show me just how well run everything is. If you don't mind. And give my horse some water."

That sort of stuck him, since he needed to be hospitable to my horse. He waved me to follow him and introduced himself as Clyde McFeed. He said we'd take a ride out together and find the camp's Woodsrider who knew everything about the work they were doing. He showed my horse to a trough where I could tie him up and showed me to his hard-driven farm vehicle, a ratty pickup truck.

We drove first to the resin still, and there were plenty of men working there, under a tin-roof nailed up to pine tree pillars. And, my God, what a smell! Just like the slimy poultice that Missus Cordelia Ephram used to slap on my leg if I got a cut that wouldn't stop bleeding. I recall seeing that black orange ooze on her fingers, stroking my skin and filling up my nostrils with wood spirits. Those vapors had made me weep.

The men at the still were lugging and pouring great barrels of the sap, which others had brought in from the forest, into huge copper kettles. There it boiled, enveloped in smoke, releasing its noxious fumes through an outlet in the cap to condense as they flowed through coils to emerge finally as turpentine. The hot rosin left in the pot was called naval stores because it was used to caulk boats. Here at the still the rosin lava and the boiled turpentine were poured into kegs and pegged up for shipment.

I didn't get into all the ins-and-outs since it was not an operation you wanted to be in the vicinity of if you didn't have to be. I'd classify it as miserably hot and stinky. The men working there were covered in black stains and smears darker than their skin, and it was not a happy looking crew. There was a white man in charge. He was labeling the barrels as they were banged shut for transport, and he gave me and camp manager McFeed a big grin, like he was drunk in the pleasure of his occupation, which he might have been.

I was relieved to get away and drive off with McFeed into the woods. We went some distance in the truck and found a whole gang of convicts, and some women whose status I did not determine, chipping away chunks of bark off the trees and nailing up V-shaped boxes to catch the sap. Thousands of trees in the forest were being worked in this way by great numbers of workers you couldn't quite see. It was shady back in the trees and quiet, save for the sound of the mallets knocking wood. You think of prisoners singing in the fields, but these folks weren't singing. They were just sweating rivers and chopping away, trying to stay alive.

As McFeed and I drove on, all we saw were more convicts chipping more trees, scalping the trunks from chin-high to knee-high, and pounding in the troughs to trap the sap. That sticky liquor bled slowly into tin cups. As these were collected they were poured into barrels, and those barrels were being loaded by strong men onto a big mule-drawn wagon.

In passing I noted how the workers' fingers were covered in the orange sticky stuff and were pasted with all the bits of bark and sandy grit they had touched. I'd have to say, these were some sorrowful looking people, and none of them appeared to be overly well fed.

McFeed was jolly, however, until all of a sudden a tall man riding high on his horse appeared through the trees to confront us. What business had we in his forest?

"That's the 'Woodsrider'," whispered McFeed, almost as a warning. Looking up from my seat in the truck, I was struck by how this

Woodsrider, with his stained khaki hat and black boots and his air of authority, reminded me of me - twenty-five years ago. Though I don't think I ever looked quite so mean. His skin was deep tan, like maybe he had some Cuban blood. He wore two pistols on his belt, and I'd never carried more than one.

He just stared, not too respectfully at what I guess was his boss, and ignored me.

"Yes sir?" he said.

I climbed out of the truck and stretched. "Nice morning," I remarked. He just shrugged.

All of the men working in our vicinity found other more distant trees to attend to and shuffled away.

"His name is Chapman," the manager said under his breath. Louder he said, "This is Gabe MacFarlane. He's the Palmers' man, come to look around." That was met by silence.

"Looks like everybody's staying busy out here," McFeed continued speaking to nobody. He looked about the thicket of trees. He seemed pleased by what he saw, most of which was wounded pines and prisoners on their knees scalping bark.

What I saw was lots of strong backs, some with scars and stripes from punishment. And rib cages like wash boards – rations would be scarce around this camp. Nobody wanted to meet my gaze, except the Woodsrider.

"Seen enough?" he asked me from atop his horse. There was also a rifle in a scabbard over the saddle.

"How long is the work day around here?" I asked politely.

"We quit when it's dark," he said. "Need to go." He wheeled his horse around and spurred her back through the pines.

"That man's always on the job," the manager said happily. "Got nearly two hundred convicts out here, counting the still and the barrel works, but mostly in the woods tapping trees. It's a big responsibility. I brought Chapman down from Georgia, where he ran a camp even bigger than this one. They call him 'Leather Britches'."

"Is that right? He's not much on conversation."

"No," the manager agreed, "but he gets the men to work, even the tough bastards who think they're too smart for hard labor. If they was so smart, why'd they become the social deviants they are?"

WOODSRIDER FRANCIS "LEATHER BRITCHES" CHAPMAN'S STORY

The prisoners who work in this camp know exactly what kind of a man I am. I don't take any flip. I don't take any slacking off. I've got a rifle, a pair of pistols, and a horsewhip, and I'll use any one of them as I please. My grandfather owned slaves in Thibodeau, Louisiana, and when they were freed my father worked those same families as sharecroppers and tenants, cutting sugar cane. Things turned sour in the Panic of 1907, and we lost the farm.

But I didn't forget how to handle labor. I was hired quickly as a gunslinger for the Galloway Lumber Company in Grabow, where they were cutting virgin pine. We put down a strike by the IWW in 1912 and killed three of them, all Wobblies, just like slaughtering hogs.

The three of us who were charged got off with the help of our Congressman, Arsène Pujo. In fact, we were not even prosecuted. But there was a lot of resentment among some people, and I moved on, with a good recommendation. I plied my trade here and there along the Florida Panhandle, following the timber mills. I had a stint with the Southern Detective Bureau. I gained a reputation for getting the job done. My position at the McKeithan Still in Laurel is "Woodsrider." Some people think I'm colored, but I'm a French Creole, and I hold colored people in low esteem. In general, they won't work without the whip and are too dumb to follow orders and respect their betters. I didn't make up the name Leather Britches myself. I took it off a dead outlaw who made the mistake of pointing a gun at me one time. I shot better than he did.

That camp manager, McFeed, had called his prisoners "social deviants." Long before I started working at Palmer Farms I had known some true social deviants. Ed Bacon was one. Charley Willard deviated as a matter of principle, or birth right. I believe the world is a better place with them not in it. But I didn't believe there could be two hundred social deviants in Manatee county who all needed confinement in a turpentine camp, and not one of them white. This whole business enterprise of rounding up poor men and renting them out to tap tree gum in the wilderness was obviously just to line someone's pockets.

But it was not my affair. The Palmers had allowed me to look over the camp, not to do anything about it. I wouldn't have known what to do anyhow. I rode away on Pardner and tried to put out of my mind the little army of ghostlike men tapping away quietly at their trees in the deep, deep woods.

CHAPTER NINE

MISTER EPHRAM DIES

Time passed. I busted up a moonshine still north of the turpentine camp that was running off a hundred jars of quality white lightening every day. I took Reuben with me. He was ready to put on a badge again, and to draw some pay, since the Palmer Farms job seemed pretty safe.

REUBEN EPHRAM'S STORY

I gave up my deputy badge the first time because I was worried about getting killed. Also, I didn't have as much heart in wearing a gun as Gawain did. There is less dangerous ways to make a living, like hiring out for farm work, and there are better ways to live, like chasing after women. A man who can graft oranges and pick grapefruit can get the jingle in his pocket, and a jingle gets a man a stool in the roadhouses, which is where the girls are. I'm a good looking gent. I've got wavy brown hair, hard muscles and slow hands. I like having a good time with good folks.

It was in such a roadhouse that I ran into Loralie Cay, who I knew from childhood up near Manatee City, which they call Bradenton now. She's a hot little number, I'd say. A redheaded lass, and I knew she used to be sweet on Gawain. I made a play for her over a glass of hard cider, but she wasn't interested in me.

"But tell Gawain that you saw me," she said. "It would be nice to catch up on old times with him."

I knew what that meant, and Gawain did, too, when I told him.

"I believe I'd best stay away from that proposition," he said, and that was it. He was staying straight at that time.

But not me. I was drawn into the rum-running business. A lot of booze was coming ashore from Cuba, and most of it was rum. They'd bring it to Key West. Then some other brave sailors would get it up to Charlotte Harbor and unload it at an out-of-the-way dock. Where some dumb redneck like me would pick it up in a car and ride the back roads north for delivery to interested individuals.

I had a fancy car, and fast. A Willis Overland Model 75. The girls loved it. It actually belonged to a certain hood I'd come to know. With the car came the job. It was great – lots of laughs, high as a kite. But hell, it's a dangerous job, too, and after I got in a couple of chases with bullets flying I decided to turn over the keys and go back to packing citrus.

To my surprise Gabe offered me a job at Palmer Farms. I think he was trying to reform me. But it came at a good time and the Farms seemed a safe place to cool off. Of course, the first thing Gabe had me do was bust up a still on Palmer property.

There wasn't much to it. The guys saw us coming and ran off in the woods. They must have just have finished their run, because the fire was dying and we heard a truck crank its motor up and spew gravel getting down the road. Someone would be happy when that load got to town tonight, but there would be a lot of overhead costs to replace the cooker we smashed up.

And that's about the most trouble we had. In my private life, I was sad when Mister Ephram died. Old man Ephram and me were like oil and water. It was always known that I was not his blood relation, but he did give me his last name and he raised me as his son. That meant he'd pull off his belt and whip me just like he would his own boys. I didn't take to that, and when I got big enough to fight back I let it be known that the whipping days were over. The other Ephram boys ganged up on me then, especially Jake who was two years older than me, and life around the cabin got to be pretty rough. Mrs. Ephram, who I called Missus Cordelia, had to make peace almost every day until I finally just moved out. First I went to bunk with Gawain in the Watsons' barn, but then I moved out on my own – doing what a young man can do to earn a buck. Nevertheless, I was sad to learn of his demise. To be honest, Mister Ephram had every reason to blister my butt. I was never an angel.

I went to the funeral to pay my respects. I was the only white man there except for Gawain. Sheriff Sandy Watson, for whom the Ephrams had worked for forty years, didn't show up. He sent word he was sick. The sermon got to be long so I slipped out.

Reuben definitely looked the part of a police officer. Sort of like an old wolf, with a checkered shirt and a brown beard, which he would trim neatly for work, and the way he crinkles his eyes and smiles though every conversation, every crisis. He wore his sidearm well, which is very important for a law enforcement officer, where almost everything depends on appearance and confidence.

Reuben always had confidence, even as a kid when he went around selling moonshine. We were raised together by the Ephrams, though as far as I know he wasn't any more related to them than I was. I'd have to say that I was more of an Ephram than a Watson in some respects, though I'm white and the Ephrams are not. They took me to their church and fixed my clothes and fed me my meals and sent me, very occasionally, to school. The sheriff didn't do that part. I never knew how they came by Reuben, who is also white, he thinks and I think. Mister Ephram never told Reuben where he came from. He just said he'd given Reuben his name, because it meant "Behold, a son." Was it by one of his daughters? An aunt, an uncle? Growing up, I never knew, but I was raised up in their large family, happy most of the time, though I slept apart, down the path in the farm shed. I got used to the pleasure of being alone at night at an early age.

Mister Ephram's first name was Hiram, but I never called him that. I called him Sir. He was strict but mild mannered. On the other hand, his oldest son, five years older than me, was an angry boy. His name was Jake, and he was angry about his station in life. At some point, Mister Ephram died, and I went to the funeral out at the AMEC, the African Missionary Episcopal Church in Bee Ridge. His wife Cordelia was there, of course, and I hugged her, and she said "You were always a fine, fine boy." Jake was there, and she said he was still working on the Watson farm, as well as running another farm he had saved enough to buy, with family support I'm sure.

Jake's face was etched with a serious frown, which was natural at a funeral but I think it was his permanent feature. He introduced me to his three children. I only remember one, a teenager, who looked just like Jake did growing up. His name was Seth. I was told that Mister Ephram named him that because it means "first grandson," which my wife, who reads the Bible, disputes. Seth never looked me in the eye. My impression was he didn't like me much.

Missus Ephram took my hand and told me, "There are some things I'd like to give you Gawain. Not today, but can you come by the house tomorrow afternoon?"

Of course I said yes. I was very curious about what she'd have. It never seemed that the Ephrams had very much, except each other.

The Ephram family lived in a farmhouse typical for those days. Four rooms with a wood-stove kitchen added on, all weathered board-and-batten on the outside, and a big front porch. In the middle of their sandy front yard – which was kept carefully swept – was a spreading mimosa tree with great pink flowers, planted there for shade and beauty. In the back was an outhouse.

Missus Cordelia, her full-length print dress covered by a yellow apron, welcomed me in and fussed about while ushering me into an armchair as though I were a special guest. She offered me coffee, which I declined, and finally sat across from me, picked up a little packet of papers from a desk, and fingered them nervously as she said, "I've kept these for a long time, Gawain. I guess I should just get this over with."

I nodded, not knowing what to expect. Taking a deep breath, she handed me an old letter, written neatly in Sheriff Watson's hand. "You can read it," she told me, so I did. It came straight to the point:

"*Hiram Ephram and Wife,*

This is my request and authority for you to look after Gawain Wallace MacFarlane, my foster son, whose parents have died tragically. There is no more room at the Watson home. The lad can be useful for any chores as you require. You are free to discipline him within reason and as needed. Gawain should be quartered in the warehouse since living under your family's roof would not be appropriate.

In addition to our existing arrangements concerning your earnings from the yield of the farm and the rent charged for your house and garden, I will pay you a dollar a week for Gawain's meals and board, and will provide additional sums for clothing. If these terms prove satisfactory for all concerned, then in the future these amounts may be adjusted as needed. I trust you will see that he gets to church and to school.

Sheriff A.S. Watson"

By school, he must have meant the one-room schoolhouse over in Rye. The Ephrams did send me off in that direction in the mornings, but I didn't always arrive as planned. The school itself was closed half the winter months for the fruit harvest and all summer due to the heat. Yet I somehow learned to read and write and count money.

This letter had not addressed any of my questions about my actual parentage, but it did somehow make the conditions under which I was raised more sensible and thought-out.

Missus Cordelia wasn't finished. She studied the other paper in her hands before resuming.

"There's something else, Gawain. I've been meaning for a long time to give this to Reuben, but the time never seemed right. I wanted to talk to him yesterday at the funeral, but he was gone so quick I couldn't. And Gawain, the sad truth is I don't know where he lives or how to get in touch with him. So I'm thinking about giving it to you."

"Me? What is it?"

"Before I say what it is, I'll tell you why 'you.' Because you're smart and have always been trustworthy, Gawain. I mean, you might tell me a story, but you wouldn't do it to hurt somebody. And because I know you love Reuben and you will know the best way to handle this. I'm getting old. It may be that Reuben does not need to know anything about his true parents or who they were. Maybe he shouldn't know. Somebody has to decide. I can't turn this over to my own children. They've all had disagreements with Reuben that have lodged in their hearts. And now Hiram has left me. I just don't think this secret should die with me."

She thrust the paper she had been holding across the space between us like it was hot, and I reluctantly took it.

Faded by age, it appeared to be the handwritten minutes of the deacon board of the Love Feast Baptist Church, which I recalled to be the little wooden chapel where Clarinda and I had got married. It has long since burned down and been planted over in lemon trees. The part of the document I could make out said:

"Brother H. Ephram is assigned the raising of the infant child, and in return shall be spared all annual tithings to the church, like sum to be deducted from Pastor's allowances."

I stared blankly at Missus Cordelia. She nodded her head as if I understood. "What does that mean?" I asked. She seemed disappointed that I didn't get it.

"Gawain, my lips have been sealed for years and years, but Pastor Dawes has long since left the church so it may not hurt none. But he was Reuben's daddy! Our church pastor!" These facts still shocked her.

My mind flipped back to when I got married to Clarinda in that same church, and I had seen a picture of that very Pastor Dawes, supposedly retired, hanging on the wall. And I had recognized him as the madman I had encountered in a different place, in a different form, a troll living in a forest called the Blackjack, as a hermit. Very possibly a murderous, cannibalistic hermit. My mind was spinning, and I barely heard her say,

"We never knew what happened to Reverend Dawes," she went on. "He just left us."

I knew exactly where he had gone, but one secret a day is enough. I had heard Missus Cordelia's secret, but I couldn't burden her with mine that would further tarnish her memory of her old preacher.

But I was wrong about one secret being enough. Missus Cordelia had something else to say to me. She kneaded the folds of her apron in her fingers. "You must realize," she continued, "that Reverend Dawes was not married to the mother of our baby, whom we named Reuben."

"Yes, ma'am," I agreed. "Do you know who the mother was?"

"I do," she said emphatically, fixing me with her still-clear eyes. "It was Beatrice Flower!"

"You mean 'Footsie'?" I shouted, jumping up.

Missus Cordelia sat back on her chair in alarm. "You know her?"

she asked.

"I do know her. She runs a . . restaurant out on Cattlemen Road."

"Is she the sort of woman that Reuben would want to meet and get to know?"

I shook my head and sat back down. "I really couldn't say." I was at a loss.

"Well, you'll have to be the judge," she said. "I've done all I can do, and I'm done with it."

I wasn't the judge. She was.

The question passed to me was, should I reveal this to Reuben or should I not? Did he even care? He was a hothead. And Beatrice Flower? I had no clue whether anyone would want to know her in that way, or what she would do if confronted with the situation. The father, Zechariah or Reverend Dawes, I hoped never to see again. In fact, I would refuse to ever cross his path. But that was me. Reuben might see it differently. My mind raced through it. I might share the burden with Clarinda. But I chose to keep it for my own.

BEATRICE "FOOTSIE" FLOWER'S STORY

I had a very churchy upbringing. My people were Holy Rollers, and we shook to the Word and crawled on the floor and spoke in tongues and afterwards ate a lot of fried chicken. That's how I remember it. I was washed in the blood and bathed in Phillippi Creek and given over to the Lord.

It's hard to say what happened exactly, but you know when you start to blossom and take an interest in boys then some of that gets in the front of your mind ahead of the Scripture. But that's not really the whole story. I met a young preacher at our church. He was just there preaching on this one Sunday, learning the job, I guess, and he was 19 years old, which I thought was very mature. Caleb Dawes was his name.

We struck up a conversation under my parents' watchful eyes, and I learned that he had very unusual ideas – about how people of all races should get together, all being children of Christ, and we should put an end to war, and maybe women should preach, too. "Why not?" he asked. I got all this in the first half-hour while we were eating biscuits and green beans in the church yard, and he captured my heart. I don't know how else to say it.

Caleb went on to preach full time at other churches, but we were hooked on each other. I'd sneak away to hear his sermons. Then I'd sneak away to hear him practice his sermons, and then we fell in love, and then I got pregnant.

There was no hiding that from my parents. I wouldn't admit who the father was. I was thrown out of their house and had to birth the child among the Africans that Caleb had taken up with. And I gave up that baby!

Caleb was shamed, too. How to admit this, but we both needed to end it, separate, break up, go our separate ways. And that's what we did and I actually lost touch. I got on a path away from the church, but I made another path for myself, I earned a living, and I learned how to stand my ground, and not back down.

The years passed. When Gawain MacFarlane came by my backwoods beerhall and suggested I might want to receive the Lord just to stay in business, he thought he was making a joke. But it touched a chord that I wanted to hear playing in my mind again.

I've always hoped that my child fared well. Lord, maybe one day I'll come out of the woodwork and claim him.

CHAPTER TEN

I EARN MY SPURS WITH BURNA LEVI

The case that earned me my points with Burna Levi was the theft of gasoline from Palmer Farms. I got to wondering how our gas pumps were metered because, for the size of the fleet, I was seeing a lot of deliveries coming from the Texaco gas company, which William Selby, another rich newcomer, owned. The deliveries seemed excessive, out of line with what I would have needed at my ranch.

By then, everybody around the Farms knew me and respected the fact that I had some sort of authority. I wasn't questioned when every evening around quitting time I checked the fuel gauges on the vehicles and read our two pumps, one gas and one diesel. Something seemed wrong to me.

I made a study of the manuals we kept in the office for all of our trucks, and this confirmed to my satisfaction that we were using up about twice what the advertised mileage was. Then I presented my findings to my boss, Burna. He was impressed with my initiative, which reflected well on the attentiveness of his department, and authorized some overtime for me to stake out the pumps after dark.

A stakeout like that was quite fine with me. It put me at work under the Florida moonlight. I've grown up enjoying my nights here in the tropics. I didn't, don't, mind doing without a fire. The moon is enough. There had never been many others I'd like as companions. Being alone was okay with me.

Darkness has smells and sounds. The wind across the celery fields. The owls. The frogs. Baying dogs somewhere. The rich aroma of plowed earth. All of it is a pleasure. In the past, if there was a moon, I might read. I could always pull out Robert Burns, and I often did that. It fit in my pocket.

There wasn't usually any resentment at home when I was away after dark. Clarinda always said she didn't care if I was home at night or not so long as I was in the bed with her when she woke up in the morning. She always left me out some supper.

Watching for the gas thieves, I didn't have any action for several nights – just foxes, bobcats and coons. I wasn't the least bit disappointed. It was May. The days were hot, but the nights were just about perfect. Refreshing cool breezes came up when you least expected, just as they might on the coast ten miles away. I could watch Venus rising, and then the moon and the stars. All very pleasant.

I knew that the pump meters were read on Saturdays, and that on Mondays the trucks came to fill them up, so the logical time to steal fuel was on Friday night. I was ready for that. With my thermos of coffee.

I wasn't even surprised at who showed up. It was our chief mechanic, Otto, and he came in driving his own truck with two big tanks in the bed, into which he commenced to pump gas in one and diesel in the other.

I watched him for a few minutes as he accomplished his theft, long enough to determine that he was by himself. Then I stepped out of the shadows and aimed my flashlight into his eyes.

He jumped, but I told him he was covered, which he was because I had my gun out. He stuck his hands in the air. I gave him two choices. He could get cuffed and ride with me to the deputy sheriff's office in Sarasota, or he could leave his truck where it was and start walking home. I believed he lived above that hardware store in Bee Ridge, which was a good five miles away, but that's the option he took. He backed up carefully, hands in the air, until he was swallowed up by the night.

I sat down and enjoyed my crime-solving until I was sure he was gone. The keys were still in his truck, and I pocketed those. Then I got in my own car, which I'd parked back in the trees, and rode up to the guardhouse by the main gate. I half expected that Flem would be gone, run for his life, but he came outside as soon as he saw my headlamps approaching. I turned my car off and walked up to him. He waved at me and lit a cigarette.

"Evening, MacFarlane," he said, exhaling smoke. His eyes flitted back and forth.

"You let Otto in, with his truck," I said, stating the obvious.

Flem spread his hands and waved his cigarette around. "Are you saying I'm not supposed to? He works here, don't he?" A perfect example of a bald-faced liar caught in the act.

"He's stealing gas, Flem. What do you get out of it? Have you been logging him in and out? I know the answer to that."

He sat down on the dirt and started to cry like a baby, keeping his cigarette in one hand. "My wife's sick," he moaned.

"Shit!" I said. "I'm going home. "Tell it to Mister Levi in the morning."

The night watchman didn't get fired, but the mechanic did. I covered for Flem. Don't ask me why - he was such a hopeless derelict is I guess the reason. Busting the great gas theft was all I needed to cement my reputation with the Palmers, and I got a raise. They even gave me a new Ford truck for driving on the job, and provided what was called permanent employment for Reuben as my assistant.

CHAPTER ELEVEN

SETH EPHRAM IS SENT TO THE LABOR CAMP

It was about a year after Mr. Ephram died (and I had not talked to Reuben about his parentage) that I ran into Seth, the Ephram grandson, at the general store. He said he was "swinging a hammer," framing new houses. He had biceps like cantaloupes. And he still didn't like me.

That was it, until one night, after I got home from Palmer Farms, I heard a car door slam outside of my house just when I was sitting down to eat with Clarinda. I went to the door and saw a figure standing politely by his Ford, giving me the chance to look him over. I made out a big man.

"Mister MacFarlane. It's Jake Ephram," he hailed me. I told him to come on up.

Jake, Mister Ephram's son and Seth's father, had white hair now. We met on the porch. He was in distress and spring-loaded like a caged wolf. And he had come about Seth.

"They say he was breaking into Mister Brewer's tackle shop in Osprey. And the judge gave him six months."

"So he's already had his trial?" I knew Jake hoped I could help, but that would be difficult once the young man had already been tried and convicted.

"Weren't no trial. Just the judge, and it was over before I even got word that Seth had been arrested. He was picked up about nine at night, and he was given his time as soon as the judge finished his breakfast."

"Did he do it?"

"Hell, no, sir!" Jake's eyes flashed. "He's got a girlfriend down there in Osprey he was going to see. She lives right near that store. He was going to visit her after work. And his mind wasn't on no fishing tackle."

"What can I do?" I asked, almost just to be polite.

"Seth's been sent off to the turpentine camp. They'll work him to death out there in the woods. That's what happens to all of them."

"Which camp? The one in Laurel?"

"That's the one. They won't let me in to see him, but I know what goes on in there. And Seth is a good boy."

He was near to tears, or to shooting someone. I asked him to sit down with me on the porch rockers and talk this situation over.

Clarinda, who had been listening from inside, brought us each out a cup of coffee.

Jake Ephram had an exaggerated understanding of my powers. But I guess I was the only person he knew with any experience in the legal system, other than his landlord "Sheriff" Watson. Who was too old to do anything. Jake talked about how good we all had it growing up together, about how he'd tried to make an honest living all these years, and raise an upright family, and get by in the white man's world. And never broken any laws. It was all true. So, of course I had to say I'd see what I could do.

"I can't promise anything," I told him, walking him back to his car.

"Well, somethin' is better than nothin'," he said. "You can't make it any worse," which was probably a realistic view to take of this unfortunate situation.

I didn't ask who Seth's judge was because I knew. It would be Jasper Braxton, and he wouldn't do a thing for me because he had accused me of having an affair with his first wife, whose name was Estelle. She was a very smart, blond-haired lady, a good horseman, and a few years older than me. She's left the state now.

And it's true. Nothing to be proud of, looking back, but I'm determined to be honest now, at least for my own account and the fire that will consume these pages. Estelle and I had first spotted each other years before, when I first rode onto Braxton's fine ranch right after we had rounded up the Sarasota assassins, after they were all fairly convicted, and before politics got involved to set them all free. That politics was paid for by Jasper Braxton, in my judgment.

But back then, the first time I was at the Braxton ranch, all I had against Braxton was that he was rich and heedless of the rights of the pioneers he called squatters on range land they had sweated over, land that he wanted. And got! He offered me a job, which I turned down. He didn't exactly say it, but the job was running off the settlers who populated our wild landscape. As I was leaving this interview on my horse Whistler, I passed the corral where his wife was working a stallion, and I blew her a kiss. Probably I did it to show my disdain for her husband. But that kiss caught her eye.

God should punish me for doing that since I had just gotten married to Clarinda, and we both loved each other, as much as we then knew about love. It was wrong to do it.

A few years later, I was in a harness shop on what's now Beneva Road – it's owned by an Amish couple now but back then was run by Jack Rudd. I was admiring a saddle when in came Braxton's wife. We eyed each other a minute, and she said something inviting, like, "You're the boy who turned down a job with my husband." It was the tilt of her head and the mean little smile that accompanied her words that did it for me. I said something to the effect that, "Your husband's a sonofabitch, and I'm glad I don't work for him." I had more ammunition, but it wasn't necessary.

We struck up a friendship immediately, browsing the leather goods together, whips, stirrups, belts and such. She mentioned that "if I was ever out driving" at such and such a time in the evening, she might be there, and I said I might be, too. And, yes, we were there. It went on from "there" for about three months.

It's very hard to say why I did this, and even harder to talk about it. But I'm trying to face up to the truth. I think I just wanted to see if I still had it, if I could still interest a woman. Some of the spark had gone out of Clarinda's and my feelings for each other. Maybe our lives had gotten too simple. Mack was a hard working young man and doing well in school. He never was a lot of trouble. It was before the Palmers, but after I had resigned as city marshal and was devoting myself to farming and real estate. Yet, the farm and my groves sort of ran themselves. I'd get busy during the planting and harvesting, but even then I was able to hire help and still make money. I'm trying to explain to myself why I was actually bored and dissatisfied with the comfortable place I had reached in my life.

Something more than boredom ought to be to blame for being unfaithful to your wife. I admit it. It was very exciting to do something wrong for a change, after always doing what was right, and it was physically exciting just being desired and touched by Estelle.

She was a beautiful woman, younger looking than her age. She had a fulsome body and shapely hips, and a wicked smile. I'd like to think that the devil was involved, but I honestly believe that it was some uncontrollable urge that came over me. Out in the piney woods, we parked our cars and looked each other over. She got a blanket from the seat beside her, like we were there to picnic, and we walked back into the trees, both knowing where this was headed. I could have stopped it all right there if I'd been a better man, but it was as if I were under a drug. I just knew how good her body was going to feel.

We spread out the blanket, and she said, "I'm glad you came, Gabe." It was the first words either of us had spoken.

I couldn't make a reply. I reached out and put my hand on her cheek, and she folded into my arms, pressing her breasts against my chest. Our hands moved over each other. She ran her fingers into my hair and pulled my head down to kiss. Her taste was strange and new and wonderful. We sank to our knees on the blanket and tugged at each other's shirts until we had them half way off and I could take her white breasts in my palms and kiss each one like a hungry baby, which in a way I was. She gasped and rolled her head back. I was so thirsty for her I couldn't stop. But I did. For a moment. I pressed her shoulders down to the blanket and kissed her mouth while I pulled up her dress. She moaned. Her panties were wet.

Estelle was an active lover. She broke free of my kiss and got her hands on my belt buckle and went about the business of stripping off my jeans. There was no doubt that I was raring to go. She could see that, and liked it. Taking matters into her own hands, Estelle pushed me down and mounted on top of me. She guided me into her, and I got a firm grip on that beautiful white fanny of hers with all ten fingers, and we gave ourselves over to pleasure. We both went to town in various ways for what could have been minutes or hours, we were too drunk on each other to care, until we had damned near drained ourselves dry.

After that experience, we had to meet each other again, and we did several times.

But I felt so ashamed. I started to get the idea that Clarinda was onto us, and I didn't want her to be hurt – or even made sad – by me. What finally broke the spell was I came home one Saturday afternoon, probably still smelling of Estelle, and Clarinda asked me where I'd been. I told her I'd been over at Reuben's helping him fix his car, which she probably knew was a lie. "You missed Mack's baseball game," she said, and walked into the next room. I stood there, feeling terrible. Mack had gotten involved in our little neighborhood baseball team, and it was important to me to go out and root at all of his games.

"This ain't working," I told myself. "I'm letting the wheels come off."

Estelle and I had arranged to meet again, so I went as planned. We parked alongside each other in the woods, again, but as soon as she looked at me the smile left her face.

"I can't do this anymore," I told her.

"Well, Gabe, I'll sure miss you." Saying no more, she got back behind the wheel, backed it up and drove away.

I had expected something a little more dramatic, but maybe that's just how Estelle showed her broken heart. Wrong, I reminded myself. That's just the way Estelle is.

I know I was the sonofabitch who got us into the affair, but I do think I was capable of more tender feelings than Estelle was. Or maybe not. I know I abused Clarinda's trust, but maybe I was also callous toward Estelle. Rough on her? In my feverish state of mind, there's no doubt I was rough. Later on, when I heard she had moved away, I was relieved.

ESTELLE BRAXTON'S STORY

I always thought Gawain was a pretty boy, tall and strong, yes, but pretty. When we saw each other in Rudd's saddle shop, he introduced himself as Gabe, so I called him that. I would have called him anything he wanted. I was starved, and he looked good enough to eat.

My husband Jasper Braxton is a cruel and ruthless man. He uses love as a weapon, withholding it until I beg. Even then he might sneer and say, "Get out of my face, bitch." A truly loathsome individual, and I'll always regret that I married him.

I turned my big smile on Gabe, admired the saddle he was looking at, touched his fingers by accident, and that's all it took.

We were passionate. We met in the woods. We met in old barns. He gave me a starfish he'd carved out of cypress and strung on a ribbon for me to wear around my neck when we made love. I used him up as fast as I could because I knew he wouldn't last. Our secret affair was tearing him up with guilt, and he put an end to it.

And I went meekly home to Jasper, damn his eyes!

Our short relationship had ended, though Clarinda remained suspicious for months. Fortunately, Estelle left town. The Braxton people let it be known that he had divorced her and she had got a lot of money and moved to California. It's funny, to me, because one of the Sarasota assassins had told the same tale years before – Bidwell said that his first wife went away to California. I have no desire to go there myself, since people don't seem to ever come back.

Because of all this, I did not think my direct appeal to this particular judge to show leniency to Seth Ephram was going to have a good effect. I talked the situation over with Burna Levi, my boss at the Farms, but he said he was powerless to help. The turpentine camps were ruled by their own laws and had their own legitimacy directly from the county sheriff who leased them his convicts. None of our business, said Burna, though he could see why there was some family connection. He didn't pry into that, because, race relations being what they were, he didn't want to get me or him involved in helping a guilty colored man, even though back in Chicago it wouldn't look so bad, blah, blah, blah. I think his bigger concern was that I was just passing as white, and he asked me that directly.

"Hell, no!" I told him. "My family is Scottish. And my wife is as cracker as they come." I didn't confess to him that I had been raised in a black household. And my cracker wife hated "race hypocrites," which was sizable part of our population.

That left me with no option but to try a direct but dangerous approach, and I drove back to the turpentine still.

The same guard asked me the same questions at the gate, and then abandoned his post once again to fetch the manager. I drove my truck in, right behind his. Mr. McFeed came out from the shade sweating and said he was surprised to see me again. I explained that my business was to visit one of his prisoners on behalf of his family. McFeed wasn't pleased with this request. There was a lot of hustle and bustle around the still, which was gushing boiling hot resin into a trough where it cooled a bit on its way into casks that were so big it took two men to bung them up and two more to help lift them. As a team, those men muscled the great barrels onto a dolly which they had to roll over to a railroad car waiting for them on a spur track. From there an engine would come to pull the cars out to the main line. Everything was in high production just then, with all the steam, heat and stench that characterized the whole works. McFeed asked if I couldn't do this another day, and I replied that I promised to make my visit short.

"Well, I can't leave just now," he told me. "I'll let you go back in the woods with Stubby." He whistled for Stubby like you'd call for a dog, and a dirty, paunchy, short man appeared from behind the still, wiping the chemicals off his hands and face with an oily rag.

He trotted forward. "Yes, suh!" he shouted. The guy was white, I'm fairly sure, and the way the boss explained the mission to him made me believe that Stubby was slow witted. But he was enthusiastic about taking a ride in the truck, and he hopped right onto the bed of mine. When I got in the driver's seat Stubby leaned over me and pointed his finger right past my nose and said, "That way!"

With him as my guide we snaked back through a system of rutted pathways barely wide enough for the truck. Finally, he pounded on the roof and said, "Walk from here!" All the trees had buckets hanging from them, collecting sap. I could hear hammers pounding chisels somewhere in the far woods.

"Do you know where Seth Ephram is working?" I asked him slowly, making sure that he knew who I was looking for.

"No. We have to ask Mister Leather Britches. Beep! Beep!" he said, gesturing toward the horn.

I took the point and blasted out a couple of "aoogahs." Stubby giggled as the birds and squirrels fled. Presently the Woodsrider, Leather Britches Chapman, came trotting through the trees on a sure-footed mount and reined up in front of my fender. He glared down at me from his saddle while his horse blew snot in the air between us.

Stubby jumped further back in the bed of the truck for protection.

"Howdy," I said, and introduced myself again.

"I remember," Chapman replied, which, other than, "Seen enough?" and "Need to go," were the only words I'd heard him speak. This Leather Britches had some jet-black handlebar mustaches, and I judged him to be a hard-worked forty year-old. The grime of Florida's sand prairies had worked into his dark skin and the creases around his eyes.

"It's hot enough today, ain't it." I said.

He sort of smiled, showing a gold front tooth.

"I stay in the shade," he told me.

"That's best. I need to see one of your prisoners." We were indeed shaded by the canopy of the tall trees. It was shadowy, but it was airless, too. "A man named Seth Ephram. He's been here about two weeks."

"See him? He's a darky and don't receive visitors."

"That's why I'm here. He's a friend of the family. We want to see to his care."

That got a laugh, delivered to the treetops. "He's working to death, like every man here." It was like the keen of the devil.

"He's only got a six month sentence," I shouted over his horse's face, "and we want him back in workable condition. I'm sure he's learning some lessons out here, but we don't want them to be permanent."

Chapman wheeled his horse. It was tight, among the pines. "Follow me," he shouted and trudged deeper into the woods. Stubby just wiggled his fingers at me, as in "goodbye," and didn't budge from the safety of the truck. I followed the Woodsrider on foot. I was armed just as he was.

After a hundred quiet yards winding through the brush we reached a crew of men plying their enforced trade to a large grove of pines. They were all shirtless and sweating because it really was hot. They heard us coming and were silent as we passed among them. I looked from man to man as I walked the path behind Chapman's tall horse. Some wouldn't look up. Here one did, with a grin. Here were stony cold eyes watching me with indifference. I saw no curiosity about who I was. They were intent on their tasks and carried buckets of sap to a cart. I heard the grunt, "That's eighteen," intended for someone else's ears.

Chapman's horse plodded past where Seth was working, but I recognized him, standing upright with a full bucket of sap in his hands.

He knew me, and shook his head as if clearing it. I hadn't seen the boy in a couple of years, but he looked half-starved. I walked up to him.

"God, please help me," he whispered. Chapman must have noticed that I'd found my man, because he turned his horse and rode back quick.

"Is that him?" he asked.

I nodded. "You doing okay, boy?" I addressed the prisoner.

Seth stood up as straight as he could. "Yes, sir, Mister MacFarlane. They're treating me alright."

"Getting all the food you need?"

"Yes, sir."

"We're counting on you coming back to work with us when you've done your time."

"I'm looking forward to it, sir."

"That's it then," I announced loudly. "Okay, Chapman. I've seen him. I can find my own way out. But remember. I want him to leave here in one piece."

I turned and hiked away, giving the Woodsrider a good look at my back. The men who had only stepped out of my way before now stared at me with a bit more interest since I wasn't accompanied by Leather Britches.

Stubby was asleep in the truck, but he woke up when I got in.

"All okay?" he asked.

What do you say to that? I dropped him back at the still and had a brief chat with the manager McFeed, who was all lathered up about some problem with his caulking crew.

"We want that prisoner, Seth Ephram, to return home," I repeated to him. "He don't need exceptionally easy treatment, but he does need to come home when he's done his time."

"What else would you expect from us?" McFeed asked, aggravated.

"Nothin'." I drove out of there. I pondered whether I should have offered Leather Britches a few bucks extra to see to Seth's survival, but the gesture might have been refused and could perhaps have marked the prisoner for special torments.

SETH EPHRAM

I never cared for Marshal MacFarlane growing up because to me he was just one of them. My grandparents had a place in their heart for him, since they said they had fed and cared for him as a boy, but my father Jake never liked him much, either. The way daddy told it, Gabe MacFarlane got special treatment. It's plain as your nose that the only reason he could be a lawman and we had to be common labor was because he was white.

Gabe treated me okay, I guess, when he'd hire me sometimes to pick his oranges, but I didn't like the way he watched me, like he expected something extra from me. Just because I was an Ephram. But I didn't owe any

MacFarlane anything. I'm the same way about Reuben, who was actually raised as an Ephram along with my daddy. To me, Reuben's not kin, and he's white, and he hasn't ever done a thing for me. He did offer to shake my hand at the funeral. I took it, but I didn't like it. I've never understood how Gabe or Reuben fit into things. But I do know where I fit. I'm a convict.

I doubt there's a God. If there was, Leather Britches would be burning in Hell this very second. Daddy told me to stand up for myself, be a man, but that don't do any good in a prison camp. They beat and starve me just for not grinning like a fool and saying "Yassir!" loud enough. And daddy can't do a thing to help.

The food here is pitiful. The molasses rots your teeth. The grits are full of weevils. There's no mail, so my girl can't write. If she's still my girl, I don't know. We was gonna get married, at least I thought so. I didn't tell her that. How I wish that I had. By now she might have run off with any one of half a dozen boys I can name. A woman can't be expected to wait forever.

I thought I had a good mind, but I'm losing it out here. It's hot all the time. We stink and we sweat in the woods and stink worse at night in the barracks they pack us in. At least the stink helps keep off the mosquitoes. There's a couple of whores in camp, and the overseers pass them around – to whoever's kissed the right white ass or who has a little money coming in from outside. Anything that would give a poor man any pleasure or reason to go on living costs money. Same here as in the real world. And that's what I ain't got. You think they'd send a white man out here to work? That's not the way this deal works, hoss. That's not the way this life works. Any white boys here, they're on the payroll.

I took some encouragement from seeing ol' Gabe MacFarlane walk into the pine trees to check on me. He's a big shot who wears clean khaki shirts and has that way about him that says, "I'm somebody. Listen up." I don't trust him farther than I can spit, but if salvation is ever to come, he's the only one who can bring it.

CHAPTER TWELVE

NOT MUCH GETS FORGIVEN

Leaving the turpentine camp, I drove the long way home, back through Sarasota, having determined to make a call on Marshal Bixby Hodges. He'd had the job for about six or eight years, ever since I resigned from the post. In my opinion Bixby was too quick with his nightstick, on the take, and dumb as a stump, but we were cordial to each other. His little office was in City Hall, which was on the Hover Brothers' dock at the foot of Main Street. It was a grand building with two turrets and flags flying on top and it was home to their popular tourist arcade, and also the city fire department. It was also the biggest boat dock in town, and the Hovers had bought it from the town mayor, Harry Higel, who had bought it from the Florida Mortgage Company when all the Scotsmen bailed out of Sarasota.

Bixby wore a white shirt and a brown tie, and one good thing that can be said about him was that he didn't stray about the streets causing trouble when he had the option of being available to the public sitting comfortably in his office which was, of course, over the water in one of the prettiest places in Florida. He greeted me warily and shuffled aside some wanted posters to offer me a chair. I told him about the Ephram boy and said I was concerned about him out at the McKeithan Still in Laurel.

"What am I supposed to do about that?" Hodges asked, not unreasonably. "He was sentenced by Judge Braxton and we ain't got room for any long-term prisoners in the jail."

"Well, I'd like him to survive his sentence," I said trying to hold his eyes.

"They treat 'em alright out there," Bixby insisted, looking away. "If he was in the Manatee County camp he'd be on the road gang. It's boilin' hot on the road, Gabe. Many a nigger has passed out and died. At least in the woods, it's cool."

It wasn't cool in the woods – it was airless and roasting - but I let that pass. "Maybe he could be a trusty, around the jail," I suggested.

"Now, Gabe, I got all the trusties I need, and why am I supposed to do you a favor?"

"I don't know. Maybe because I've sat in your chair."

"Not in this chair, Gabe. I got the county to buy me a new one. I didn't care for sitting in your chair. There was always some question, MacFarlane, about whether being raised with the colored people - you were or you weren't. Know what I mean?"

"No, I don't, Bixby." I was starting to get hot.

Hodges smiled, but his beady eyes got beadier. "Your mama and daddy both died young. Only Sandy Watson seemed to think he knew who they were. And he let you get raised by niggers. That's what I mean."

I stood up. "Bixby, you're more of a dumb cracker than I thought you were. While your papa was sucking your sister's pussy up in Missouri or wherever you came from before you moved to Englewood, mine was killing Yankees for Robert E. Lee, so go screw yourself."

I stomped out, aware and embarrassed that my efforts on behalf of Seth Ephram could well be producing negative consequences. Maybe I should just go and impound Seth myself, I thought. Ride out and grab him with pistols blazing, like in the movies. Heroic, like in the Last of the Mohicans, which I'd taken Clarinda to Bradenton to see, our one and only motion picture adventure. A wiser plan was to discuss this again with Burna Levi and see if he would reconsider and bring some Palmer pressure to bear.

CLARINDA KNOWS

I knew about Gawain's affair with Estelle Braxton just as soon as it happened. My husband was usually an easy going fellow. Very serious about his work, be it wearing a badge or setting out garden plants, but, maybe because he saw so much trouble and disagreement in the world out there, he was always kind and humorous at home. When I got mad or upset about something he'd smile and pat my rear and make a joke about how he'd better hide the guns before I shot somebody. That settled me down, mostly. We'd go to church. We'd talk about what happened during the day. We got along well. That's the way it's supposed to be, I always thought.

I've calmed down a lot over the years. Two miscarriages will do that to you, and raising a boy who likes everything there is to enjoy in the country – hunting in the woods, fishing in the creek, even helping me with chickens and his dad with the oranges, riding horses, chasing the country girls.

Gawain and me brought up Mack to be a good young man. He was never a great student, but he's willing to work. His pa wouldn't let him give me any sass though Wallace is, by nature against authority. He comes by that honest from his father. Gawain likes to be the man who is the authority. He doesn't like kissing anybody else's ass.

All in all, I thought we had what a marriage was supposed to be. I know I get depressed some days, but I held onto the life we had.

One day Gawain came home at the usual time, but instead of giving me a hug and a twirl he looked past me and went to the sink to wash his face and hands.

"How was your day, honey?" I asked him.

"It was alright," he said, using the dish towel.

"Anything happen?"

"Nothing special," he said, and right then I knew there was something wrong. In the back of my mind I figured it had to be a woman. And I had a pretty good idea which one it was.

The next morning, he said he had to go to court and put on his uniform shirt and pants. Which I had pressed for him. I asked him which court was he going to.

"Judge Braxton's," he said – probably the first name that came to his mind.

When he left I looked in the paper and saw where Judge Coxswain was sitting in for Judge Braxton who was away at a judicial conference in Tallahassee. That immediately told me all I needed to know. I'd seen Estelle Braxton give my husband a sweet smile at a holiday courthouse party the year before, and seen him blush. I poked him in the side then, but where was I going to poke him now?

Whether I wanted them or not I got a few more details from a lady friend of mine from church. Noreen keeps her nose to the ground, and she shared with me the fact that she had seen Gawain driving east toward the Myakka River and not even waving when he passed. And a little later here comes another car with a woman behind the wheel – something you didn't see too often back then. The woman was by herself and had a white scarf wrapped around her hair. It covered the lower half of her face and was blowing in the wind, said Noreen.

"Nothing strange about wanting to keep out the dust," I replied with a smile, but I knew, I just knew.

"That's true," Noreen said and patted my knee.

I wasn't completely positive it was Estelle Braxton, but whoever it was could drive a car. That's when I made up my mind that I would learn how to drive, too.

I say things had been good, but let's be honest. You're married a long time, and you lose interest in some things. I think you know what I'm referring to. Over time I became used to Gabe's affections, and I guess he became used to mine. When you're used to somebody you don't see how they're changing, or how much they want to change.

I always yearned for some education. I wanted to be more a part of world events, all the things going on in the world. I wanted to make my own money, even if just a little bit. I wanted indoor plumbing, let's be frank. And I wanted a car you could start without taking a chance on breaking your arm. My dissatisfactions might have little to do with Gabe, but I was down-deep mad at him for not paying more attention to me and the things I wanted.

Maybe he felt the same way about me, and that's what drove him into another woman's arms.

I wasn't going to make any scene. I made up my mind to watch and wait. After two or three months I could tell it was over. His disposition in the mornings got brighter, and he started talking to me more. He also started taking a drink in the evenings. I didn't say much about it. I'd drink too if I was as guilty as him. By mutual consent, which neither one of us said out loud, we stopped having intimate relations. And that went on for quite some time.

I became fixed in my determination to do some more with my life than iron a man's shirts and put supper on the table. I imagined that this was probably the way my Mama felt when she made up her mind to leave Pa and just disappeared into the night. I hated her for that, but now I'm not so sure.

About a year after all this sordid aggravation happened, as I was starting to get over it, we heard that Judge Braxton and his wife got divorced and she moved off to California.

Gabe has always liked a drink. He'd get tight once a month or so with

Reuben Ephram, who had moved over to Grove City where he could find more interesting things to do than pick oranges. Gabe would go over to Reuben's "for a game of chess," on Wednesday nights when I went to church. And he'd come home bowlegged sometimes.

That drinking picked up after Estelle left Florida, or maybe it was because Mack went into the Army and off to the War. We were both worried about him, naturally, and with our young man gone maybe his dad didn't need to always set a good Christian example.

The funny thing was, when I started getting into the Anti-Saloon League, through our church, Gabe supported me. He'd even toss a few dollars into the bucket. He said he didn't see anything wrong with a man having a drink or two at home, but he didn't think saloons were healthy.

When I started talking about women getting the vote, and going to suffragist meetings and picnics, he'd go with me. There's a lot I admire about Gawain. I admired what he did as the town constable, and I admired the work he put into our farm and our investments after he quit being a lawman. When he asked me about the offer he got to go to work at Palmer Farms, I told him it was just fine with me. Because I knew it was something he wanted to do. I couldn't hate the man no matter what he did. I'm miserable about a lot of things in my life, but I can't blame it all on my husband. But I don't talk to him about it either.

As soon as our son Mack got home safe from the War he picked up and left us once again. Mack was trained to be an airplane pilot in England, and right after the War he got a job with a flying service in Tampa, ferrying rich people back and forth to St. Petersburg mainly. With Gawain working at Palmer Farms, there was nobody but me at home and only our old dog Nero for company. I had a lot more time to think about myself, what I wanted to do with my life, and what kind of job I could do that someone would pay me for. And I had more time to dwell on my grievances, which isn't Christian.

Gawain and I went to see the Last of the Mohicans at the New Wallace Movie Palace on Manatee Avenue in Bradenton. It's a grand place. There must have been 500 people there. It was the first time I ever ate red licorice. They sold it in the lobby, but you had to smuggle it inside the theater. Gawain was excited about the big battle between the Indians and the soldiers, and he got indignant about the cowardly officer who betrayed the fort's weaknesses. I wept for the white girl and the Mohican who loved each other so much that they joined themselves together in death. We drove home lost in thought, and what I remember most is wishing that Gawain loved me like that. Maybe Gawain was looking for that kind of love, too.

My life changed soon after that. It was in the Lord's plan that I was to reunite with my mother, Lovelady, who had left home when I was sixteen without so much as fare-thee-well. I had seen her but once since then, passing by in a wagon with some man, and she had looked away. From me, her only daughter.

CHAPTER THIRTEEN

THE MURDER OF MAYOR HIGEL

I intended to discuss Seth Ephram's case once more with my boss, Burna Levi, and to emphasize again the danger Seth was in at the Laurel turpentine camp, but when I reported to work at the Farms the next morning all of the talk was about the murder of Mayor Higel.

A visionary is what they called Harry Higel, for in his three terms in the first Sarasota City Council and in his three terms as mayor, he had overseen the arrival of the railroad terminal, the building of a great hotel, the paving of downtown streets, and the construction of a five-story bank building. He was a true promoter of tourism and, as a personal venture, he had teamed up with some other prominent locals, Captain Roberts and E.M. Arbogast, to create the Siesta Land Company to acquire Sarasota Key. They renamed their prize "Siesta Key" and advertised it in promotional materials tacked up all over town, and they put home-size parcels of this beach-front property, expensive ones, on the market, advertised far and wide. Mr. Higel acquired a schooner, the Vandalia, and converted it to steam power in order to ferry people from the city dock (which he owned) across the Bay to his Siesta Key. He built bathhouses there, so that beach lovers could change into swimsuits without having to duck behind the palm trees. Then Mayor Higel built a hotel on the north end of his key, the Higel Hurst, overlooking Big Pass. It boasted of running water in each of its 20 guestrooms, gas and electric lights throughout, and a dining room that would seat a hundred. He couldn't stop preaching about the need for a Siesta Key Bridge to connect the beach with the mainland, and it was finally built. Unfortunately, his great hotel burned down a month before the bridge opened. The cause of the fire was never made known, and the Mayor just said he would march forward and build a new and bigger attraction.

The Palmer Farms office was in a commotion when I got there because Harry Higel had reportedly been beaten to death just a few hundred yards from his home on the Key, at the corner of two sandy streets he had named Higel and Siesta. My boss Burna Levi instructed me to ride back to Sarasota along with him. On the way, with him driving, he told me what else he had learned.

He said that a man named Burt Luzier had found Higel's body, early that same morning after driving over the bridge in his truck to collect a load of shells to deliver to Mr. Selby back in town for use in building the grounds for his new mansion. I knew Burt. He was a hardworking and reliable man. Burt had his son Merle with him, and the two of them had loaded the victim, still breathing, but his face and head terribly mauled - so disfigured and covered in blood that the Loziers did not even recognize him - into their truck. They carried him back over the bridge to Dr. Halton's office on Main Street. The doctor took one look and immediately ordered that the injured man be carried across the street to the undertaker's where he could be properly spread out and examined.

Burna Levi's face was grim when he told me that Higel's head was so smashed that Dr. Halton also didn't know who he was, though the mayor had been the doctor's patient for years. (Higel was actually not the mayor any longer – just the richest and best known man in town.) Only when he noticed a gold ring inscribed "HH" on the victim's still warm hand did the doctor realize that this was his friend. He quickly arranged transport for the mayor to the nearest hospital in Bradenton. Unfortunately, by the time the ambulance got to him the hospital, Mr. Higel had died.

As I heard all of this in our speeding car it was a few minutes past noon. We roared up to City Hall where Marshal Bixby Hodges' office was located and found there the county Sheriff, L. G. Wingate, and his "Investigator," a man I'd not met but who was introduced as Deputy D.R. Brown. They had just gotten back from the scene of the crime, which D.R. had searched with bloodhounds. The dogs could now be heard braying in a truck parked out on the dock. Hours after the murder, the lawmen were still visibly excited.

The killing must have occurred about 8:30 in the morning because "Mayor" Higel had taken a walk at about eight and met a "black man named Pearly," who was supposed to deliver a load of lumber to Higel later that morning. This Pearly was, at first, thought to be a likely suspect, but Sheriff Wingate was convinced he was innocent because Higel still had a gold watch in his pocket when he was discovered. This removed the only possible motive for Pearly – theft - as far as the sheriff could conceive. For his part, Pearly said that, after meeting Mr. Higel in the lane, he had gone about his business, driving off to get the lumber he was supposed to deliver. There was no blood on Pearly, and he hadn't stolen anything, so the sheriff reluctantly sent him on his way.

Investigator Brown's investigation had come up with a section of half-inch rusty pipe about seventy feet away from where Higel's body was found, and he had the pipe carried to town for "testing" by Dr. Halton. The bloodhounds led the investigator around the area, but no other physical evidence was found. However, Brown did find faint footprints in the sand, which he followed from the murder scene as far as Bayou Louise. His dogs lost the scent there. Across that narrow bayou was the house of a noteworthy citizen named Rube Allyn. In the morning's low tide one could wade, or certainly swim, across the bayou, or you could drive another hundred yards toward the pass, to the point of the key, where there was a narrow wooden bridge. It was capable of carrying a car over Bayou Louise. That bridge was private, and it connected Higel's drive with a parallel street, platted as Gulfmead, on the other side. The only inhabited dwelling on that far side of the tidal bayou belonged to the Allyns. Otherwise, there were "Lots for Sale" signs stretching far down the sandy "street" that had been newly cleared though the mangroves and palms.

Now I knew that this Rube Allyn was quite a character. He'd had a newspaper that published the sensational, and Rube could find sensation in a local church picnic or events in far-away Hong Kong, didn't matter, and he probably made up the great bulk of them. He was also a professional story teller, and had appeared on stages "throughout America," as he would say, a travelling entertainer. Allyn did have a beautiful wife, I thought, who was very patient and tolerant, which she would have to be to live with a flamboyant man like Rube. And she must have loved him because they had, I think, six kids. One of them had a handicap. He helped his dad set type for the paper, and rode about Siesta Key on a cart pulled by a little donkey.

Rube had had a famous dispute with some of his creditors, and he tried to save his printing press from seizure by floating it on a raft from Higel's old dock over to Siesta Key, but this turned out to be a poor idea since both barge and press sank in the bay. So he moved his newspaper business to St. Petersburg where he was able to print his papers after-hours on presses belonging to the *St. Petersburg Daily Times.*

The way Marshal Bixby Hodges put it was: "We approached the Allyn house with the dogs and called for Mister Allyn to come out. He did. I asked did he know that Harry Higel had been murdered. And he said he didn't." Having developed that information, Marshal Hodges and his investigator, Brown, with his dogs, drove back over the bridge to Sarasota to regroup. "Appeared to me that," Hodges added, "Rube's pants were wet."

"What do you make of that?" Sheriff Wingate asked the room.

"Don't really know," Hodges replied. "But maybe Rube killed Higel and waded home over Bayou Louise to keep from being seen on the bridge."

Wingate quickly changed the subject. "Did you happen to notice all the reporters outside on our dock?" he fumed. "This is the biggest thing that ever happened here! Killing the mayor, for God's sake! They're not going to let up till we get the murderer!"

"What is your next step to be, Sheriff?" Burna Levi asked politely. "I'd gladly assist. And so would Gabe MacFarlane."

I was glad to be volunteered because I did believe I could help. Wingate was not an ambitious man. As I judged him, he just wanted to retire richer than when he got elected, mostly by renting out county prisoners and doing favors for moonshiners. Bixby Hodges, I've already expressed my opinion about. I didn't know Investigator Brown. It takes a smart man to handle bloodhounds, so I withheld my judgment.

"Of course we appreciate the offer," Wingate said doubtfully, but he was aware of the Palmers' sensitivities when it came to protecting the upper class. "I guess since Mr. Higel was the most eminent man in town, all hands on deck can't hurt, can it boys?"

His deputies shrugged.

I raised my hand. "So why don't we go back out there again," I suggested, "and speak to Mr. Allyn, and Mrs. Allyn, and Mr. Higel's widow, and see what else we can find out?"

"That's my plan," the sheriff said. "You boys take the investigation to its next phase while I talk to these reporters and tell them what we've got so far."

I drove Burna's car, by myself, over to the Key, and Hodges and Brown went in their official city coupe with a flashing light on top.

Burna stayed behind to keep an eye on Sheriff Wingate. I think the Palmers suspected the sheriff of being incompetent, and they were also struck hard by the murder. Harry Higel had been a friend of Honoré and his mother, Bertha. They sat together on some bank boards of directors, I think, and undoubtedly had financial dealings in common.

Everyone had become used to having a bridge from the city across the Bay to the northern end of Siesta Key. Five years earlier, however, you'd have needed Harry Higel's excursion boat, or your own, to get over the water. From the end of the bridge you passed over a little mangrove island before arriving at the key itself. From that point the Higel house was just a few hundred yards further north where it was built on a spit of land that protruded into Big Pass. The trails on the key had recently been bulldozed to make them wide enough to accommodate cars. Though cars could drive on the resulting sandy roads, the thirty or so trailblazing residents of the Key were more used to walking once they got to the beach.

We turned right on Higel Lane and drove through the open gate that marked the beginning of the developer's personal estate. Up by the Higels' residence I parked behind Bixby Hodge's police car. He and Investigator

Brown were already walking over to the house, but I chose to set off in another direction. The narrow body of water called Bayou Louise flows with the tide down the middle of this tip of Siesta Key, dividing it in half like the jaws of an alligator. A wooden bridge ran across that bayou. Harry Higel probably built it, since it starts on his property. On the other side it takes you directly to the Rube Allyn home, which is the only one on the street that runs along that side of the bayou. The bridge is wide enough to fit a car, barely.

The Allyns, like the Higels, had an unobstructed view of the Gulf of Mexico, and all of the beach anyone might ever want to walk on. I strolled over the plank bridge, looking for clues. I didn't see any.

The Allyn residence was built up high on stilts, and it did not appear to be completely finished. The home was solid enough, but a side wing was still open to the elements, like so much else in our rapidly developing community.

I climbed up the steps to their wooden porch and knocked on the door. Mrs. Allyn answered.

"Sorry to disturb…," I began, but she interrupted.

"I know you, Constable. You broke up a fight in front of our old home in town one time years ago. It's terrible about Mister Higel."

"Yes it is, ma'am, though I'm not a constable anymore. I work for the Palmer family, and I'm just sort of on loan to the Sheriff's office today. It certainly is a terrible thing. Is your husband home?"

"No." She seemed distressed. It could be because there were children screaming in the background. "He's over at the Higels' house right now, offering his condolences." She breathed heavily, her neck was flushed, and I felt sorry for her but didn't know why.

"Do you know anything about what happened this morning?" I asked.

She stepped back, and I stepped forward, over the threshold. The kids were still making a racket in the back.

"My husband hasn't been himself," she whispered. "He's been acting queerly, and has been for some time. He's been so depressed and talking a little crazy."

"Thinking back, I do remember that fight I broke up in front of your house. Seems to me that your husband might have been involved in it. I definitely recall him being very worked up. Exactly how has Rube been acting crazy lately?" I smiled with as much warmth and understanding as I could muster.

She ran her fingers through her hair and shook her head. Her brown eyes seemed to melt.

"His work is enough to drive anyone crazy. He drove back from St. Petersburg last night after putting the paper to bed, as he tells it. It was so late, and he was agitated from all that driving, he couldn't seem to sleep. He just paced about. I tried to keep him quiet so the children wouldn't wake up." She smiled suddenly and tossed her hair back, as if I should know about wakeful children. Which I do dimly recall, but we only had the one child, and those days and nights do pass from memory.

"Did he leave your house early this morning?" I asked.

She thought about it. "He must have," she said, "for his morning walk, even though he couldn't have slept much. When I got up to fix breakfast, he wasn't here. When he got back he told me he had been walking on the beach."

"What time was this?"

"I don't know. It was early. He walks every morning." A child screamed behind us. "Now I must go," she said.

"Yes, ma'am, and thank you. Were you here when he came back from the walk?"

She was closing the door, but she said as she disappeared, "Of course. Where would I go? Now, if you'll excuse me."

"How long would that have been, that he was walking?" I asked, but she was gone.

"Too much happening," I heard her say behind the closed door. Then she began singing loudly, "Bobby Shaftoe's gone to sea, Silver buckles on his knees, He'll come back to marry me, Bonnie Bobby Shaftoe," a song, I guess, for the purpose of quieting lively youngsters.

From the front porch the Allyns had the western horizon and a long view south down an empty beach. One of the most beautiful spots in the world as I'm sure I've said before. It can make you believe God has a good plan for the world.

The Allyns were lucky to have such a view. Just like it was a hundred years ago. But, step by step, progress was approaching. Just as Mayor Higel had predicted and yearned for. But it had not arrived just yet.

It was late afternoon, overcast and windy, and I could see tents flapping far away down the beach. There was a man fishing in the surf and a small dark head in the water indicated someone else was swimming. I went down the steps and set off hiking in that direction.

In time the fisherman spotted me coming, but he kept up with his casting then reeling back, then casting…. He was working two rods.

My "Palmer Security" badge was glinting on my chest, so we could dispense with the normal introductory remarks.

"Have you been camping here long?" I asked, and learned he had been there for a week. The fisherman's name was Herman Rosener. He and the swimmer, who washed up in a wave, were from Kentucky, what he called "tent tourists." "Any law against fishing around here?" he asked with a worried grin. I guessed he was thirty-something and too friendly by nature to be running from the police.

"Did you know there was a murder near here this morning?" That took the smile off his face. He pulled in his hook, stripped it of bait, and set it in the rod's eyelet.

"I don't know anything about a murder or anything like a murder," he said slowly. He brushed sand off his elbows. "We're just here for a vacation from the snow."

His friend came up, shaking off water. He grabbed a towel from the sand. "What do you want?" he asked.

"There was a murder of a man, this morning," I repeated. "Where were you fellows at about eight o'clock?"

The swimmer, whose name I heard as Rodman, piped up with, "I was fryin' fish and scramblin' eggs right over there." He pointed at a dead fire in the sand. "We're living and loving the healthy life." His hair was blond, almost white, and his skin was burned red by the sun.

The fisherman nodded. "We were up quite early," he said. "Very early. But trust me, we didn't kill anybody."

"Understood, but did you see anyone? Did anyone see you?"

The swimmer shook his head. The fisherman started to, and then said, "Yes, there was a man walking on the beach, right after sunrise. Maybe 7:30. I didn't notice much about him, except…"

"Except what?"

"He was tall."

"Tall? What was he wearing?"

"Brown pants, and his shirt was, I don't know, maybe white."

"Which way was he going?"

"Same as you. Going south. He walked by, didn't say anything, and I didn't pay any more attention to him. I don't know where he went because I was minding my own business."

"Would you recognize him if you saw him again?"

"Mister," the fisherman said, "I couldn't tell you if he was thirty or fifty, had a beard or a mustache, or was clean shaven. That's the way it is."

"How'd you fellows get here, by the way?" I asked. "Did you drive over from the mainland?"

"Nope," Rodman, the swimmer said. "We rode the train all the way from Paducah to Sarasota, and we hitchhiked from the station out here with our gear."

"How long do you plan on staying?"

"A few more days, if that's alright."

"You don't need my permission," I told him. "I hope you're enjoying the beach." I left them and walked away from the water toward the dunes. It was a very windy afternoon on the beach, but the clouds far overhead sailed along in no particular hurry. It was the kind of day when a storm can pop up out of nowhere. Puffs of foam scattered along, some snagging delicately on a clump of seaweed or one of the millions of white shells that lay as a carpet on the beach before blowing away and disappearing. Even through my khakis I could feel the sand peppering my shins.

Climbing up to where the sea oats, cactus and seagrapes guarded the dunes, I found that a new road had been plowed through nature's garden. Following it to a wider cut, a future thoroughfare, I saw no houses in view, but parades of red and white surveyor flags indicating that newcomers were expected. Wandering a few more hundred feet I reached an intersection of these new roadways that had been marked with street signs to explain where I was – at the uninhabited "Shell Road" and the uninhabited ending of "Gulfmead Avenue." But of mangroves there were plenty, bordering numerous wet spots in the terrain, though the roadway had sliced away quite a lot of them. On Gulfmead Avenue I noted vehicle tracks, running north back toward the Allyn home. I was interested in the tire marks, of course, but they appeared to be about as common as any Ford would make. For no particular reason I turned inland, and quickly came upon a car parked off to the side, among a grove of cabbage palms, with no soul around it. There was, however, a pile of cigarette butts on the ground. I noted the license tag number, "LTV 30" from Pinellas County, and continued ambling along, on the lookout for the owner.

Another cross street, I forget the name, appeared, and I made my left, which took me past the marshy end of Bayou Louise, itself surrounded by a jungle of mangroves. I intended to make the circuit back to where I was parked at the Higel house. There were more red and white flags stuck in the sand every fifty feet or so, meaning that lots, however soggy they might be, had been surveyed and were ready for sale. I was seeing nothing of special interest, just swatting at the bugs, when I was surprised by, of all things, a donkey, pulling a cart on Higel Avenue, and in that cart was a young man who yelled "Whoa," and stopped in front of me. "You would be?" the fellow asked.

"I would be Gabe MacFarlane. And who you would be?"

"I would be Lewellen Allyn, printer, publisher and typesetter."

His legs were crooked and small, but he had as man's torso, and a bushy head of brown hair. The donkey gazed placidly at my chest.

"Is your father Rube Allyn?" I asked.

"The very same," he declared proudly.

"And would you have any idea who killed Mister Higel?" I asked.

"No, haven't seen any strangers here," the young fellow said – or maybe not so young. I couldn't be sure of his age. "What a terrible thing to have happen around here, don't you agree?"

"I certainly do. Where's your father" I asked.

"Home, probably. I've been exercising Ulysses and getting some sun." He yawned.

"Do you know anything about that car over there?" I pointed back through the trees.

"I didn't see any car. I didn't see anyone," he said.

"Where were you this morning about eight o'clock?"

"Eating my breakfast, I guess. Dad brought us home late. We were still printing the paper well after dark."

"That's so? Printing it where?"

"In St. Petersburg. It's a long drive back."

"You were with your dad the whole way?"

"I'm always with him."

"Were you with him this morning when he went for a walk on the beach?"

"Guess not," he laughed. "Mom woke me up after nine, and Dad was in the kitchen."

"He was seen on the beach at 7:30," I submitted. "Short night's sleep for your dad?"

"Don't know about that. That man, Higel, was quite a bad neighbor."

"Oh? And why was that?"

"When we drove home last night we found that old Higel had closed his gate so we couldn't take the short cut over the bayou bridge. Dad had to back up and turn around in the sand. We had to drive the long way around here to get across the bayou to our house. It annoyed Dad, who was tired as a dog."

"Did it annoy you?"

He thought that question was funny.

"Don't know what you mean," he said. "I just work for Dad, but I was tired as hell when we got home."

"About what time, you said?"

"Sleepy time," he responded. "Got to go." He flicked his reins and his donkey woke up and started pulling the cart along.

"Bye," Lewellen called.

I waved at his back. He and I were going in the same direction, but halfway back to the Higel home he pulled off into the woods and I didn't see him again.

At the Higel house, where I had parked, I found out that deputies Hodges and Brown had driven off and left me. The lady who answered the door said she was Mrs. Higel's sister and that the sheriff's men had taken Rube Allyn into custody.

"They say he had blood stains on his pants," the sister said, "and the pants legs were wet where he swam over the bayou after killing poor Harry."

Thinking I had better catch up with events, I jumped back into the driver's seat, spun the car around, and sped back to Sarasota. I drove past the spot where I had seen the car parked in the woods. It was gone. All of my investigative prowess, in other words, didn't seem to be making the least bit of difference.

CHAPTER FOURTEEN

MY LIFE CHANGES ON
THE DAY HARRY HIGEL DIED

There had never been such a mob scene in Sarasota! A least one hundred people, many of them armed, and not just men but women, too, were clamoring for Rube Allyn's blood. They had City Hall surrounded. I had to park two blocks away, and people were running down the sidewalks to join the commotion. I got among the throng and pushed my way up to the building, where I made my presence known by beating on a window until Marshal Hodges saw me. He cracked open the door, and I slid in.

Sheriff Wingate and his deputies, now numbering four, were huddled around a desk outside Rube Allyn's cell. Burna Levi had gone elsewhere to report to the Palmer family. Allyn was seated back in the shadows. I couldn't see his face.

"You can note for the Palmers we've got us a mob," Wingate observed. He was speaking slowly, like his mind was busy someplace else.

"It's getting bigger," I reported. "You'd better go out there and try to talk them down."

"I've thought about that," Wingate said, "but I can't say as I like the idea." He had a cigarette, unlit, between his fingers and he rolled it around until it broke, spilling bits of tobacco on his pants.

Marshal Hodges piped up, "You gotta remember that those people out there are voters, but this end of the county didn't go for Wingate. They're liable to string him up."

"Then you go out there, Bixby," I suggested. "You're the Sarasota City Marshal."

"Not my job," Hodges said flatly. I saw Wingate frown, undoubtedly disappointed by the lack of support he was getting from his team.

"Well, you've got to do something!" I yelled, trying to be heard above the rowdies outside who were beating on the door.

The sheriff stared at the floor. "I'd feel a whole lot better if we had this boy up in Bradenton," he said. "Those are my people there."

"And what about Rube?" I demanded. "Did he confess?"

"No," the sheriff said sadly. "Marshal Bixby Hodges here arrested him on the basis that his pants, which Bixby found on the clothesline, were wet and had red stains on them."

"And don't forget the pipe I found," Investigator Brown chimed in. "And the tracks in the sand my dogs followed that went in the direction of Allyn's house."

The suspect's voice came from the cell, loud and clear. "I didn't do it! This is preposterous! I'm being set upon by fools!"

The pounding on the door was getting louder.

"Better get Allyn out of here," I advised.

Wingate looked around at us and rallied to make a decision. "Each of you boys take a shotgun," he said clearly. "We'll take Rube out the back and jump in the cars. Then we'll drive right through those people – if we run over a few toes we don't stop - and get ourselves and that prisoner to safety."

The deputies gathered up their weapons. They pulled Allyn out of his cell and put handcuffs on him.

"You coming?" Wingate asked me.

"No. I'll go out front and try to draw their attention. That should work for about thirty seconds so you had better move fast."

The squad of them got ready to hustle out the back door, and when Wingate pulled back the bolt I opened the front door and stepped into the mob outside.

I held up my hands, asking for quiet though someone yelled , "They're surrendering," and cheered.

I shook my head and hollered, "Listen to me. The law is going to take care of . . ." That's about as far as I got into my speech before a man somewhere in the crowd noticed the police cars racing from behind City Hall and yelled, "They're getting away!"

The people ran from in front of the building and streamed after the cars, but Wingate and his deputies had made good their departure for Bradenton.

I went back inside the Marshal's office and locked the door behind me. I'd been left alone and in charge, the first time that had happened in many years. So I poked around.

There was the oak desk, of course. Hodges might have replaced my chair, but not the desk. I had sat behind it once, as the man with the silver star, and now I did so again. The desk had little drawers on both sides and a long one across the top. I scoped them all out. Mostly paper clips, but I did find an interesting packet tied with a string. It contained a number of folded papers, like letters, which I took the liberty to unwrap and read.

These were handwritten ledger sheets, titled "Prisoner Payroll." Lots of names, with dates of "Incarceration," and "Sentence Release Date," and "Employer," and "Fee." I had found the roster of leased convicts!

That last item was the most interesting. The "Fee" for each prisoner for each month was generally $20. I did some math on that and it came down less than a dollar a day, a little more if you took off Sundays to pray. Generally free-world wages for backbreaking work in the hot sun in our part of Florida were running $3 a day for the lowest grade of employment, so I could see why renting prisoners was a wise move for employers, though one has to consider the cost of starving them to death and putting a leaky tin roof over their heads.

I was surprised to see that Bixby had 131 prisoners to account for. I had no idea that there were that many miscreants in south Manatee County. But as I reflected on the attitude of our Circuit Judge, Jasper Braxton, I could see how this easily might happen. I wondered who was collecting that fee and where all the money was going. Twenty dollars a month times 131 prisoners was a lot of loot.

This was all so enlightening that I prowled through the other drawers, and the big one under the desk top. There were Bixby's commendations, nice notes from his mother, and a photograph showing him, with his bushy mustaches, and his wife and five children all posed in front of a quilt they must have hung on the side of their barn for the occasion. That was touching, and it made me almost like the man.

The photograph dulled my appetite for further snooping, and I locked the place up. Outside City Hall the wharf was now empty of all our angry citizens. It was past closing time anyway. I walked back to Main Street to recover my car, but, for some reason, another one caught my eye. Right in front of the bank was a Ford that looked like the one I had seen before. And the license tag number confirmed it, LTV 30. It was the same car that had been parked out in the bushes on Siesta Key, a few hours after Harry Higel was killed.

I peered into the windows. The car was locked, and I didn't see anything inside but some papers on the seat - face down. The bank itself was closed. I asked a couple of pedestrians if they knew who owned the vehicle, but no luck. I found a spot under the awning of the jewelry store across the street and waited in the fading sunlight for half an hour. No one showed up.

I was tired and went home where, it turned out, I had problems enough of my own.

LOVELADY BARLOW'S STORY

I saw my long-lost daughter Clarinda at a women's suffrage lecture at the Presbyterian Church in Sarasota. We women hoped to push our state of Florida to ratify the Nineteenth Amendment and put it over the top, but of course this is a very conservative area and many people, even a lot of Christian women, think that it's the man's place to be in charge of all things earthly and the woman's place to be concerned with the spiritual and do as she's told. But the purpose of the meeting suddenly became unimportant. As an active volunteer I had been seated up in the front, on this little stage they have in the fellowship hall, though I wasn't one of the speakers. I'd say about thirty-five ladies were in the audience, and then I saw her.

Looking around the room as our chairman repeated the speech I had heard her make numerous times before, I saw Clarinda in the fourth row. I was sure it was her though it had been more than twenty years. At that moment her eyes fastened on mine. They got wide. She put her hand to her cheek and started to rise, but caught herself and sat back. I stared away. As I had done once before. The sadness washed over me, and I could almost feel the heat of her disappointment and anger. "Lovelady," I told myself, "you're old enough to take some heart-ache now." We both waited out the lecture, knowing we would have our confrontation.

After the clapping, prayer and adjournment for punch and cookies, I walked up the aisle as she was coming down. We met in the middle and I put my two gloved hands out to her in meek supplication. She took them. I teared up, but not her.

"I was wrong. I always knew it was wrong," I said, almost sobbing.

"Of course you were wrong," Clarinda said, drilling me with those beautiful eyes of hers. "You left me and Pa in the middle of the wilderness without a word. What kind of mother is that?"

That hurt, but I said, "Yes, but you look well. I'm so glad to see you, and I want to hear about your life."

"Enough of that," she cut me off. "Where have you been? Why'd you leave us?"

My mouth opened, but nothing came out. "You've got some explaining to do," Clarinda stated and marched me outside. She sat me down on a little bench in the park by the church to hear my story, to extract it like a dentist does a tooth.

The story I told her wasn't exactly the way it happened. I made it a little more romantic. Everybody is entitled to a few secrets. As I started to speak, the sadness completely overwhelmed me.

"I was just so depressed out on the farm," I said, trying not to cry. "We had travelled so far, and we were still just so poor, and I didn't see any way out." I took a deep breath and continued. "I got to thinking about an old beau of mine from back in Georgia named Garland. I started wondering what had happened to him in life. And then, I wrote him a letter. I shouldn't have done that, but I did." Clarinda was watching me intently, skeptical expression and a frown on her face, but she was nodding to keep me talking.

"I addressed my letter to him in care of the little country church we both attended, and I kept it in my apron pocket for about a month, thinking I should just throw it away. But one day one of those cowboys came through.

I gave him a couple of cold ham biscuits and a drink of tea, and he said he would mail my letter when he passed a post office in town. I was relieved in a way to have it gone. I didn't want Pa to find it. That would have been too traumatic for him. I never expected the letter would get to Garland or that anything would come of it.

"But six months later, there he was. Garland. Waiting in the barn for me one morning while Pa was out plowing. I heard the cow making a racket and went out to see what the matter was. And as soon as I laid eyes on the man, something just came over me. He took me in his arms, and instead of struggling I just melted. Pa would have shot us both if he'd come walking in. He certainly would have. But Garland got away before we were discovered. And then a week later he came back, as he said he would. We met in the woods, and I felt like I couldn't go on living without him. I couldn't stand being with your Pa anymore. So I ran off with Garland."

"What about me?" Clarinda shouted. She startled the mockingbirds above us and away they flew. I could see she was ready to slap my face.

I couldn't do anything but burst into tears when she said that. The truth was, I had put my own hopes and dreams above those of my daughter's, and there was no way to wash that sin out of my hair.

What I managed to tell her, crying, was, "I was younger then than you are now. I was afraid of being an old hag farm woman, and dying with nothing to show for my life but worn hands and a bent-over back. I'd never had any fun..." That's when I broke down and just blubbered.

To my surprise, Clarinda took pity on me. Her face softened, and she asked, "Well, momma, did you ever find any fun?"

I dabbed at my tears with my shirt sleeve, and then told it to her straight. "Yes, baby, I had some good times, and some hard times. And things are getting better now. You see, Garland had a ranch on the Braden River, and his wife had died. He had two children by her, and he needed help with them and the ranching. We were happy for a time. I tried to give those kids what I stole from you. But something happened to him. I don't know if it was another woman somewhere, or him feeling guilty about us living in sin, but he just withdrew from me. We stopped talking. The boys began to find jobs in town, and the house felt empty. Making a long story short, I left him. You might say I'm sick of men in general. There's very few I have any use for."

Clarinda smiled at me sweetly. She seemed to understand. "What are you doing now?" she asked.

"You mean when I'm not waving a sign that says, 'Give Us The Vote?'" I laughed, though I wished she'd call me Mother. "Why, I have a little sewing shop, honey. I live upstairs all by myself. It's in Pinellas County. It's a lively area, too. Lots and lots of rich Yankees and their wives and their maids. There's even a big bunch of single men who always want to talk about their sail boats. Some of them even say they're in favor of women's rights. You don't meet those guys in church, girl, but if you try, you might get them to go with you to hear a good sermon."

"I thought you said you were tired of men," she persisted.

"I am. I'm just wondering about you," I told my daughter. "You know, I'd love to have you come and stay with me."

135

CLARINDA DECIDES

My mother was telling me my own life's story. That's how it sounded to me. Can dissatisfaction with the whole marriage . . . thing . . . be passed on from mother to daughter? My mother had done what I was now thinking I ought to do. Of course, I wasn't out-of-control in love with anyone like she had been with this Garland fellow. I might look at an attractive man now and again, and a few had definitely hinted that they'd like to give me more than a polite peck on the cheek, but I had never gone there. As my mother told it, passionate love had made her inflict the cruelty of abandoning me when I was barely sixteen. Mack, my own child, was grown, so my leaving home would be no cruelty to him. It wouldn't break Gawain's heart either. That's the sad part. I know it would hurt him awful bad, but it wouldn't break his heart.

I needed to do something though. I needed to feel new and free. And have some fun.

Leaving downtown Sarasota and the Higel investigation in the rear view mirror, I got home that evening after dark, expecting to smell dinner cooking on the stove and the coffee boiling. But instead I found a stack of cold pots. There was a note on the kitchen table. I opened it, knowing something was wrong.

"Dear Gawain," it read. "I've gone to visit my mother and will be in touch. Love, Clarinda."

Didn't that beat all!

CHAPTER FIFTEEN

RUBE ALLYN DENIES IT

Clarinda did not return overnight, and the next morning I arrived at Palmer Farms in distress. There was good phone service there, but I didn't know anyone to call about my missing wife except Clarinda's friend, Noreen. And she claimed to know nothing. But she sure did want information from me - though she didn't get it. I forced myself to laugh at her inquiries and wished her a good day.

I thought about calling our son Mack up at the Tampa airfield, but I decided it would be unwise to get him involved in something that would probably blow over in a day or two.

Seeking to find relief in work, I called the marshal's office to get an update on the Higel investigation. Eventually I was put through to Bixby Hodges. "Did you get Rube Allyn up to Bradenton all safe and sound?" I asked. I'm sure my tone was as surly as I felt.

"We had no problem with that," he snapped.

"When I was out on the Key yesterday, I saw a car. It was parked in the palmettoes."

"So?" He was surlier than me.

"Yeah, well, why was a car parked there? I didn't see any driver. I talked to two fellows fishing on the beach, and it wasn't theirs. So whose was it?'

"You tell me."

"Maybe you can tell me. The license tag number was LTV 30. And after you arrested Rube, when I came back to leave, that car was gone."

"So what?"

"It's a clue, Bixby. A suspect." Bixby was dense, either on purpose or born that way.

"I don't see it," he said. "Siesta Key is open to the public. Lots of people visit. We've got Rube Allyn in custody. The sheriff agrees that Allyn did it."

"Based on your report and your arrest, Bixby."

"And what's wrong with that?"

"You may be ignoring other possibilities."

"Goodbye, Gawain." He hung up.

Usually he called me Gabe. Saying my full name meant something to him, but it was nothing I cared to dwell upon.

Clarinda didn't come back that night either, or the next day or the next, and it was not until a week later that I got a postcard from her. It was a picture of St. Petersburg Beach. All it said was, "I'm doing fine. Love Clarinda." If she'd written anything else on the card the whole neighborhood would have known about it, but her message didn't do a thing to satisfy my curiosity. Strangely, I wasn't too worried about her. She was an extremely capable woman. And I wasn't even lonely, not at first. It was sort of relaxing.

They kept Rube Allyn locked up for about two months in the Manatee County jail in Bradenton. Finally, a grand jury was convened. The jurors reviewed the evidence, or lack of it, and let him go. The prosecutor had nothing to show but a few whiffs of suspicion. There was no blood on Allyn's pants or shoes according to the scientific analysis. The red stains on his pants, Allyn testified, were from red ink he'd splashed while he was printing his paper. There was no blood, nothing but rust, on the lead pipe Inspector Brown had found near Higel's body. There were no witnesses to the murder. No weapon was produced. The two beach tourists had gone home to Kentucky, and they wouldn't have added anything except that they saw a tall man walking that morning. Sure, it could have been Rube, but he said it wasn't him. Rube claimed he was still in bed that morning, exhausted from getting his newspaper to press and making the long drive home from St. Petersburg. That was a different tale than what his wife had told me, but she didn't testify to the grand jury. Naturally, the contradictory statements made me suspicious.

It was purely by the Grace of God that Sheriff Wingate's deputies, Bixby Hodges included, hadn't arrested the poor shell contractor, Pearly, who encountered Higel walking down his lane shortly before he was murdered. A similar lack of evidence might not have saved Pearly, and he likely would have met his Maker at the end of a rope.

I knew that Sheriff Wingate blamed Bixby Hodges and his other deputies for their investigative stupidity, but it was the sheriff who would pay the price. There had long been a movement simmering in Sarasota to break loose from the "Bradenton Crowd" and have a county of our own. The fact that the Sheriff Wingate couldn't nail anyone for killing the most popular man in Sarasota was the straw that did it.

Rube Allyn was released in March, and an election where "South County" citizens could vote on their secession from Manatee County was set for May. The campaign was hot, and the turnout was large by local standards. More than six hundred votes were cast, and they favored creating the new county, with Sarasota as the county seat, by almost five-to-one. Of course, only people in the proposed new county were allowed to vote. In Englewood it was unanimous. All twenty-five voters favored leaving Manatee. The same in Myakka City, where all seven electors voted their independence. The only hold-out was the town of Venice, which went 30 to 22 in favor of staying, and that probably had something to do with some Northerners who had invested heavily in property there and feared change of any sort.

So, a new county was formed. Sarasota, the town and the county, were on the map. The politicians had to work fast. A government had to be formed, and it was left up to the Governor of Florida to select the men who would run things until fresh elections could be arranged. The only office of any interest to me was who was to be our new County Sheriff. Naturally I assumed it would be the City Marshal, Bixby Hodges. But the Palmers got busy. They had all sorts of clout up in Tallahassee, and they got their way about many things. And one of those was the appointment of the first Sheriff of Sarasota County: Burna "Heinie" Levi, my boss. He took office on July 1, 1921, and I came along with him as his first deputy.

Bixby Hodges, of course, wasn't too happy about this. He kept his peace in front of Burna, but he let me know just how little he thought of me.

"You ought to have retired a long time ago," he griped when no one could hear.

"I did retire," I reminded him. "But I wanted to come back just so that I could trouble you, Bixby."

REUBEN EPHRAM'S NEW JOB

Gawain came over to my house one Wednesday evening while his wife Clarinda was at church, or so I thought. This was a couple of months after the excitement about Harry Higel's murder had died down, and I'd been wondering when Gawain would turn up. I heard he'd gone back to work as the chief Deputy Sheriff in Sarasota, and I thought maybe that's why he had made himself so scarce.

He had been my regular Wednesday night chess opponent, unless I had a sunset fishing cruise chartered that day. You see, I quit Palmer Farms after being rehabilitated there for six months because I was bored to death. Problems of any substance, Gabe would handle, and all I was doing was drawing a paycheck. But I left on good terms.

My new line of work, if you can call it that, was to take our plentiful visitors out to catch fish – particularly fish that put up a sporting fight and took a good picture when you landed them. I cleaned our catch for the customers. Redfish, snook, and pompano. We did tarpon sometimes. I've had men who wanted to tangle with sharks, just for the hours of contest these mighty opponents could give you. On a bad day we could still catch mackerel and trout, but that's not a really bad day, you know. A truly bad day is when you get run back to the dock by a storm in the Gulf and don't get paid.

I can fish any day of the week. I just like to do it. My boat then was a 20-footer, built locally, and paid for with the money I had earned at Palmer Farms. It had a two-cylinder Evinrude. I could take four people comfortably, as well as me. The only drawback was the cost of gas. But people paid well, *and I'd take couples out for a cruise to see the stars over Stump Pass or Lemon Bay, or just to watch the white and brown pelicans nest. Everyone had a grand time.*

My customers could have all the drinks they wanted. That was one of my specialties. It ain't fun if it's legal, I'd say, then and now. They might live the straight-and-narrow in Worcester or South Hadley, but when they came down here for a Southwest Florida vacation they could live the high life with me. I could get anything for them. Bottled in bond? I could provide that, and I'd drink what they'd paid for and forgot when they wobbled off my boat. They also left behind their catch, for me to clean. My life then was as free and easy as you could want. I think Gawain, or Gabe as he started calling himself, liked getting out of the house for a chess game more than he did sipping whiskey with me, but we did tend to hoist a few when he showed up. After his lengthy absence, I was happy to see him pull into my driveway at last.

I know as little about what makes women tick as any other man, but I was stunned by the news that Clarinda had left him.

"You two are compadres," I protested. "Are you nuts?"

"Me? Hell no! She's the one who left."

"To where?"

"To be with her mother, wherever that may be," he said.

"Then you need to go find her."

Gabe got quiet then. Finally, he said, "I believe I will have a drink, since you asked."

I knew that our Wednesday evening "prayer meetings" as we called them had been somewhat disagreeable to Clarinda, but he didn't have to answer to her at the moment. So I obliged his request. But what I actually asked him was, "Are you two having, you know. . . "

"Not as much as we used to," he admitted, "We've been married a long time, Reuben."

"Then maybe the two of you need a break. It could be for the best," I suggested.

"I'm having a break. It takes some getting used to though."

"Do you want to meet some women? I know a few single ladies."

Gabe was shocked by the idea. "I wouldn't have a notion how to act," he said. "In any event I ain't ready to be disloyal to Clarinda."

"Would you like me to ask around about her?" I inquired. "Like where she is. I know a lot of people in my business,"

Gabe shook his head, like he was the one in charge of this situation.

"Reuben, I also know a lot of people in my business. I'm a goddam policeman!"

"True, but your marriage is falling apart. If you start looking for her, the word gets out. I can be more private about it."

Gabe shrugged, which I took as a maybe. The man was clearly miserable. Like a frog on the highway, he didn't know which way to jump.

Reuben was correct that being newly made an official deputy sheriff gave me the opportunity to investigate many things, and when my head cleared in the morning what I decided to investigate was the Pinellas County vehicle registration records. I called up the courthouse in Clearwater and inquired about tag number LTV 30. I had plenty of time to read a stack of advertising circulars while waiting for the answer to my question, but when the clerk got back on the line she gave it to me. "That car tag was issued to the Noel A. Mitchell National Detective Agency," is what she said.

That put a big grin on my face! Surprises like that make being in law enforcement fun.

Most everyone had heard the name Noel A. Mitchell because he was the mayor of St. Petersburg. More than that, he was widely known as the inventor, chief executive and marketer of the famous "Mitchell's Atlantic City Salt Water Taffy." This candy was carried in every tourist store in Florida, and Noel Mitchell's picture was stuck on the label of every jar. Mitchell also called himself the "Sand Man" in advertisements for his thriving St. Petersburg real estate business, and those ads were printed in newspapers all over the country - wherever sand-starved suckers might reside. But I didn't know he had a detective agency.

I took this information to my new sheriff Burna Levi. Though he showed little interest in my phantom car or anything having to do with Noel Mitchell, he did say that I could "pursue it."

I pursued it first with Bixby Hodges who told me bluntly that I was kicking a dead horse. His loud opinion was that Rube Allyn had killed

Harry Higel and had gotten away with murder! And his job was on the line about it! Case closed! But I couldn't let it go. A great man, by our standards, had been beaten to a bloody pulp, and nobody had to pay?

I drove over to Siesta Key to see what the recently exonerated major suspect, Rube Allyn, might tell me. I found him packing up all his belongings. There were boxes and even chairs and personal heirlooms on his porch. In his yard was a pick-up truck loaded with household furniture. I parked beside it and got out.

Rube appeared on the porch to see who I was, and I hailed him.

"What do you want?" he asked, squinting into the sun.

"Deputy Sheriff MacFarlane, sir. You might remember me from the lynch mob at the jail."

"I do remember you," he said. "Why the visit? We're quite busy here."

"I see that." I approached the porch. He didn't invite me up the steps, so I addressed him from below. Someone had planted cactus as a border to the walkway, but they weren't particularly pretty. "Are y'all moving?"

"Yes, we are," he shouted to the wind. "Do you blame me?"

"No, I guess not. Nearly getting hung and spending two months in jail for a murder you say you didn't commit is reason enough. Where are you headed, sir?"

"None of your business is it?" he asked. His son Lewellen, the one who rode in the donkey cart, appeared behind him in the doorway. He was supporting himself with two canes, and baggy pants covered his legs and probably braces.

"I always thought you got a raw deal," I told him, walking closer.

"They never had any real evidence."

"That's a striking thing for a lawman to say." It relaxed him a little.

"I'm an honest kind of lawman. I can't say that for Bixby Hodges. It was him who persuaded Sheriff Wingate to have you arrested and charged." The son, Lewellen, disappeared inside the house.

Rube Allyn shrugged. "Water over the dam," he said. "My reputation is ruined. My business is shot. I live next door to the widow Higel who believes I beat her husband to death. Just chaff in the wind."

"You were poorly treated, no doubt about it," I agreed. "I do have a question for you though. It's why I drove out here. There was a car stuck back in the palms near the beach the morning Higel was murdered. It's registered to the Noel A. Mitchel National Detective Agency. Do you have any idea what that's about?"

"Noel A. Mitchell? Why he's my dear friend." Allyn came down the steps. I thought he was about to start something. The man was younger than me, but he had silver streaks in his mane of black hair. He was tall, with a strong jaw and a red face and looked like he could have been a prizefighter.

"That's the same Mitchell who's the mayor in St. Petersburg, right?" I went on.

"Yes. And you say his car was on the Key, down here, on the day Higel was killed?"

"I saw it here."

"Noel Mitchell and I had dinner together in St. Pete the night before Higel died. At a steak house. Then I went back to work to get the paper out. Then I drove all the way home. It took a couple of hours. There's no reason that his car would be here."

"Maybe it was driven by somebody else, somebody who works for Noel Mitchell?" I suggested.

"He's got some cops work for him," Allyn said thoughtfully. "They spread out on jobs. I don't know. Nothing to do with me, I'm sure. Why, if I know Noel, he went out to have a few drinks after we parted. Probably sold half a dozen beach-side lots."

"Are you two in any business together?"

"Nosy, ain't you?" Allyn reached in to his pocket like he had a gun but came up with a purple handkerchief. He blew his nose loudly. "Noel is my friend. He advertises in my paper. He is the greatest promoter St. Petersburg has ever had, if you didn't know. He's got green benches all over the city with his name on them. Now, if you don't mind, I've got work to do."

"Yes, sir. Thanks for your time." If I'd been wearing a hat I would have tipped it.

Allyn took the porch steps with long smooth strides and disappeared inside. He certainly played the aggrieved suspect flawlessly, but he looked powerful enough to have pulverized the face of his neighbor, if that was the sort of man he was.

I went back to my car and got behind the wheel, killing a few moments while I pondered my next move in "pursuit" of my suspicions. Perhaps I would drop in next door and intrude upon Mrs. Higel. According to Rube, she was still living in the home across the bayou.

Lost in thought, looking out over the waves rolling into Big Pass, I didn't see the donkey until his head was almost beside my face! It startled me good. Thoroughly surprised, I stared without humor as the rest of the miniature pet passed and the boy reined up right beside me.

"I heard what you said to my dad," he whispered, though there really was no need. A breeze had kicked up from the water that would have whipped away any words we exchanged. "You said Pop didn't do it."

"I said he got a raw deal. What do you think?"

"I think that there's things, and then there's things," this peculiar character said with a smile. Not that I knew what he meant, but I nodded.

"Here's a thing." He held up a blue steel pistol and pointed it right at my chin. I ducked in the driver's seat and contorted myself trying to get to my own revolver.

"I'm not going to shoot you," he laughed. "I don't know how."

Slowly, I peeked back over the door and saw that he had lowered the weapon.

"Let me see that, young man!" I ordered. He reached through the window and dropped it in my lap willingly.

It was a Colt .32 six-shooter, what they call a "Police Positive Special." One of its hard rubber grips was missing, and it was fully loaded. The safety was on, thank God.

"I found it," Lewellen volunteered

"Where was that?"

"Out on Siesta Drive. In the sand. Yesterday. I didn't know what to do with it."

"Good thing I came over here today, Lewellen. Handing it over to me is the right thing to do. Did you show this to your father or mother?"

"My mother? No, she doesn't like guns." He laughed again.

"And your father?"

"Sometimes he gets coocoo." The boy twirled his forefinger around. "He once shot the ear off an owl."

"He did what?"

"That's what he told me. Shot it right off."

"Wouldn't want that," I agreed.

"Nope," was his reply, and he slapped his donkey on the haunch. The cart rolled away.

There was a lot more I wanted to know, but didn't think this fellow was the one to tell me. Rube emerged onto the porch, and gave me a look conveying he was angry to see I was still there.

That was enough for me. I had that gun, and I was going to roll. I stepped on the ignition. No spinning of tires. But I backed out of my spot, turned around, and cruised as fast as possible on the packed sand roads back to the Sarasota bridge.

CHAPTER SIXTEEN
A VISIT TO NOEL A. MITCHELL

I got that gun directly home. The place was empty, as usual. Just my dog Nero who barked at me like I was a burglar and then wanted food. I was hungry, too, and there was a steak in the ice box getting older by the day, but first I had a task.

I owned a fingerprint kit, bought through the mail in response to an advertisement in the Police Gazette. There had been no previous excuse to test it except on myself, which I had done to see how it worked.

The kit had found a place at the top of a bookcase that also held Clarinda's curios, several books she and I had accumulated about birds and wildlife, a Methodist hymnal, my Dictionary, a chess and checkers set, and a pile of National Geographics which we, she, subscribed to.

Intent on collecting evidence, I brought down the kit and laid the gun out on a clean dish towel. I admired it for a minute. I did not see any traces of blood, but it was certainly scratched up. The gun was loaded, and one pistol grip had broken off. One of its fragments was still there, held fast by its retaining screw. Otherwise, the firearm looked serviceable, sandy, but well oiled.

I took the bottle of powder from my kit and did what I'd done in the test, gently brushing the fine black carbon dust over the gun handle, the exposed frame where the grip was missing, the chamber and the trigger. I saw nothing but smudges, and that was disappointing. Between Lewellen and me both handling the gun, however, the smearing was probably inevitable.

A smarter detective would have started at the barrel because that's where I found the prints. There were sworls and ridges everywhere. The gun had been held by the barrel. And used as a cudgel against Harry Higel's head and face or I'd be a monkey's uncle! That was my excited conclusion. I saw a whole set of prints, with the pinky closest to the sight, so the weapon could be used as a club. The thumb print was way over to the right side, so I figured it belonged to a left-handed man. Or woman, I suppose.

I used the clear tape that came with the kit and laid it, bit by bit, over the most precise prints I had detected. Lifting each tape off gently, I stuck it in the designated space on the cards I'd been provided. They were labeled "Evidence," and I repeated this process as long as there was a print left to lift. Then I stowed the revolver in an empty cigar box I had handy, packed up my kit, and sat back in my chair quite satisfied, speculating on how the gun had got in to the sand, how the boy had found it, and, if it was the murder weapon, why the murderer might have tossed it away. But I liked these questions, as I always had when on the hunt, and celebrated a little. The bourbon disappeared, and the steak got fried.

Though I slept peacefully, I had a swell headache when I woke up.

After downing a pot of coffee I drove to the station in Sarasota, where Sheriff Levi was present, and I described my findings. He looked pained. Pointing out the obvious, he reminded me that Noel A. Mitchell was a mayor, thus a political figure.

The mystery car I'd seen on the Key? Who could explain that?

"We already had one botched investigation," Burna said sourly, meaning Bixby Hodges' arrest of Rube Allyn, "and we don't want another."

Sheriff Levi was actually much more involved at that point with another crime in which a lot of money had gone missing. There had been an embezzlement at the First National Bank, where many rich Sarasotans including the Palmers kept some of their money, and in the Palmers' case, sat on the board of directors. The sheriff was preoccupied with solving that crime.

He was distracted, but to his credit his concluding words were, "Okay, you're a bull dog, Gabe. You can call Mayor Noel Mitchell and find out what he has to say about this."

I understood that "call" Mayor Noel Mitchell meant "call on" the gentleman, so on Sunday, when Clarinda would normally have woken me up for church, I hit the road before daybreak and drove north to St. Pete. It's a long drive. I calculated it at three hours, at least. Up the Trail through Bradenton to Tampa took about two, and then a big swing north, west, and south to get up, over and around old Tampa Bay. A man named Gandy was in the process of building a bridge across it, but he wasn't finished yet. I took a five gallon can of gasoline along with me for the ride, though I was sure there would be stations along the way. It's just I hadn't made that trip in a few years and wasn't certain what to expect.

The new highway, called the Tamiami Trail, had just been completed close to us. It was an asphalt paved road now running all the way from Tampa to Fort Myers, and they were still working on building it south and east across the state to Miami. I was looking forward to getting the feel of the new road, and I even wore a jacket and tie for the occasion.

It was a fine road, and I ate up the miles. New mobile home parks and roadside attractions – the "Crazy Mirrors House," "World's Largest Alligator," and "Monster Man 100 Feet" – had sprung up like firebush. When at length I reached St. Petersburg it was late morning.

Now even then St. Pete was a big city. Far bigger than Sarasota. There were several towering hotel buildings, and even though it was Sunday, the streets were busy with tourists. City Hall was closed, but for miles I'd been seeing billboards for the "Sand Man Realty Company" and had no difficulty finding Noel A. Mitchell's real estate headquarters. But to get there you had to drive, very slowly, through his "Tent City."

One of the mayor's innovations, I came to learn, was to offer a municipal park for tent campers and provide them with free garbage pick-up and toilet facilities. The object was to generate tourism in St. Pete, and it was working even better than anticipated. There was a sea of campers. Tin cans, Airstreams, pup tents, and circus tents, hundreds of people, all parked and crammed together beside the highway on the north side of town. They were within easy walking distance to downtown's hot dog stands and seashell businesses and a short drive to the beach. They had it all for free, plus sun and sand. Why would they ever leave?

Outside of Mitchell's land company there was a row of green benches for the comfort of pedestrians, and inside there were posters of quarter-acre lots, or tenth-of-an-acre lots, for sale. Two girls and one guy sat at their desks waving, ready to serve me. I asked the first one in the row for Mr. Mitchell. I explained who I was, and she rose gracefully and went behind a door to check with her boss.

I was soon ushered into the Mayor's "office" where I found his eminence eating a sandwich and wearing a big napkin tucked into his collar. He stood up to greet me, wiped his chin with the napkin, and tossed an empty French's mustard jar into a trash can as he dusted off his hands to shake mine. He was a tall man with receding hair, wire rimmed glasses and a mouth set in a sneer. He didn't look at all like the handsome wavy-haired fellow whose picture was on the Salt Water Taffy box. He was more like a flush-faced county prosecutor. There was a glass on the desk full of ice and some brown liquid – could have been Coca Cola or tea.

"What brings a Sarasota County Deputy Sheriff all the way up to St. Petersburg to see me?" the mayor asked politely.

I told him I was looking into the death of Harry Higel.

"Is that so?" Mitchell said. "Seems like that should have been done before they put my friend Rube Allyn in jail for two months." He sat back down at his desk and pointed me to a chair.

"I agree with that, Mayor," I said, watching him crumple up the butcher paper wrapper his sandwich meat had come in. He threw it in the general direction of the can but missed. "I think there's some loose ends Sheriff Wingate overlooked."

"That's no surprise," Mitchell said, extracting a toothpick from behind his ear and starting to put it to use. "How's my friend Heinie Levi like being the new Sarasota County Sheriff by the way?"

"He's got a lot on his plate, but he's doing fine," I told him. "And I have to admire all the business you've got here." We were making friendly.

"I'm selling St. Pete, the finest city in Florida. It's the easiest thing in the world to sell. But I've also unloaded this old place." He waved his hands to show that he was referring to his real estate building. "Come back in a few years and you'll find a ten-story office edifice that Perry Snell is going to put up on this very spot. I sold him this whole block. We've got a coliseum going up down the street and some elegant and major hotels on the way. You might think about investing here."

"Progress everywhere," I said, encouragingly.

"Yeah, our town is constructing a 'Million Dollar Pier and Casino' out into the Bay as we speak. Sarasota can't beat that. So what are these loose ends you mentioned about the Higel case?" he asked, getting down to business.

"There was a car with the license plate LTV 30 out on Siesta Key the day Mr. Higel was killed."

"And?" he prodded, pleasantly enough.

"It's registered to the Noel Mitchell Detective Agency. I'd like to know what it was doing there."

That quickly, he started to sweat. "Who says one of my cars was there?" He wiped his forehead with a napkin.

"I do. I saw it parked off the path in the sand not half a mile from where Mr. Higel's body was found. I went to question Rube Allyn about the murder, and when I came back the car was gone."

"Well, I sure didn't drive it there," Mitchell said angrily.

"Okay, who did?"

"Most likely Billy Neal. He's one of my detectives. Maybe you've heard of him?"

"No. Why would I?"

"Why? Because he's got a reputation as the best pistol shooter in Florida, that's why! He competes at fairs all over. Nobody can outshoot him. Maybe he was down there for something like that."

"There weren't any fairs in Sarasota on that day. And another thing is, we found a gun somebody seems to have lost in the bushes not too far from where Higel's body was found, a .32 Colt Police Positive."

That struck a nerve. "Harry Higel was not killed with a gun!" the mayor shouted.

"True enough," I agreed, "but he could have been beaten with one. Have any of your people mentioned losing a Colt revolver."

The question bothered him, and he took his eyes off mine. And he shook his head. "I need to wash my hands." He sprang up and opened a door behind his desk to a little room in which I could see a sink.

"Where might this Billy Neal be?" I called after him. "I need to talk to him, of course." Noel didn't close the door, but he had turned his back to me while he ran the water. I took my chance and retrieved the mustard jar from the trash can and slipped it into my jacket pocket. I got a sniff of his drink. It wasn't Coca Cola or tea, but a product from Kentucky with which I was familiar.

"Billy's over at Indian Rocks Beach working on a burglary at somebody's winter house." Noel dried his hands and came back to his desk. "I don't expect him back for another hour or two."

I told the mayor I'd wait. He said he had business to attend to out of the office, and I said no problem, I'd just walk around St. Pete and grab a bite somewhere.

Mitchell stood up abruptly, signaling that our meeting had ended. He didn't offer to shake hands so I left.

My car was parked on the street nearby, and I had been lucky to find the space. There was a hustle and bustle about St. Petersburg that we hadn't yet seen in Sarasota. I deposited the stolen mustard jar under my car seat, then strolled down the block taking in the atmosphere. New construction was everywhere. I thought about walking down to the bayfront where the tourists would be plentiful but instead settled upon getting something to eat at a diner on 4th Street named Splendid City.

I slid into a red-upholstered booth, and a pretty waitress brought me tea. I ordered the meat loaf special. It was a nice place, clean, and had quite a few customers including a mother who was trying to bribe her kid with French fries to sit still. My food came, a big slab of meat plus green beans and mashed potatoes and gravy, and I was just settling in to enjoy it when in walks a man I pegged for being Billy Neal.

I surmised it was him because he looked every bit the private detective. First off, he was wearing a suit that built up his narrow shoulders. Then he sported a skinny black tie and a wide-brimmed Panama hat parked with a cocky attitude on his ferret-like head. And he had a face you'd love to punch.

He slid into the booth, across the table from me. I could tell he was packing something under his jacket on the right side, so maybe he was left-handed. He immediately removed any doubts I might have about his identity.

"I hear you're looking for me Mac...Farlane, is it?" He fastened me with a threatening stare. For some reason I didn't feel threatened.

"You must be Billy Neal, the famous sharpshooter."

That almost made him blush, but he toughened up and said, "That's me. So?"

"So, you were on Siesta Key the day Harry Higel was beat to death."

"I don't know about that. And that doesn't mean anything. There are lots of people out there."

"No, I didn't see that many. And not driving cars. Mostly it was cops. What were you doing there, Neal? It's a long way from St. Pete."

"If it's any of your business I was seeing to a client who was having some trouble with his wife."

"Who might that be?"

He had practiced for this one. "I'm not at liberty to say."

I laughed out loud. "You've been waiting to use that for a long time, haven't you? Private detectives don't usually come into Sarasota without so much as a how-do-you-do to the local sheriff. What were you really doing there?"

"I told you, it's none of your damn business. And I'd like to know what your authority is to be questioning me in St. Petersburg." He picked up the butter knife from the place setting in front of him and started spinning it around on the table. He noticed me watching and carefully put the knife back in its place.

"But then you threw away your gun, or did you just lose your gun. Why'd you do that?"

"Now you're talking crazy! I've never lost a gun in my life! You're just reaching for smoke."

"I bet it's the same model that's in your holster right now."

"Go to hell!" he said.

"The grip was broken off, probably because the revolver was used to bash in Harry Higel's skull."

"Wait! Where's your proof for any of this?"

I took my napkin, reached across the table, and pinched up the detective's butter knife. He reacted too late to stop me. I smiled at him and placed the napkin and knife on the red upholstery beside me.

"Fingerprints don't lie," I told him. Then his fist did come across the table. I caught it in mine and we struggled for a quiet moment over who got to keep his hand. "I've got a badge," I whispered. "How about you?"

Billy disengaged and slid out of the booth.

"You're an asshole, and you better watch your back," he hissed.

Having sufficiently menaced me, Billy Neal departed the restaurant, pausing only to say something to the waitress at the cash register.

My meatloaf was cold, but I went back to eating it anyway. The waitress came over.

"That man says you're swiping my silverware," she said.

"I am taking this knife," I admitted. "I'm a deputy sheriff and I need it for evidence. I expect to pay you for it." I pulled out my billfold and handed her a dollar bill, which was about twenty times what the knife was worth. She pocketed it.

"How's your meal?" she asked.

"I think I've had enough of this," I said pushing away my plate, "but, tell you what. I believe I'll have a slice of that peach pie and a cup of coffee, black. What's your name, ma'am?"

"Wouldn't you like to know."

Turns out, her name was Germaine.

I was in no hurry to leave.

Driving north out of St. Pete to skirt around Tampa Bay before turning south again for the long haul home, I passed through a lot of rural countryside. Home sites in cabbage palm thickets and dilapidated orange groves were for sale everywhere, of course, but there were still working citrus and pineapple farms, still wind-blown scrub prairie and still sandy dunes. The road is lonesome in the late afternoon, and I was followed the whole way by a black car a quarter-mile back. Billy Neal, no doubt. My own gun was under the seat, but I left it there.

I had no idea what he might be planning, if he had the brains to plan anything. Right before you hit the Hillsborough County line there's a long dark stretch of road through a big patch of woods owned by the guy who founded the Oldsmobile car company. It ended at the Tampa Road, and you hook a right at the stop sign. I made my turn, but in my mirror I could see the car trailing me circle around the stop sign and point back toward St. Pete. Was it Billy Neal, or maybe a local cop?

163

Who knew?

I got home to Sarasota at a decent hour, just before seven with the sun sinking low, road weary. But I set out my fingerprint kit on the kitchen table and probably went through a tablespoon of powder dusting off the mustard jar. There was a nice thumb and probably a middle finger deposited there by Noel Mitchell. As carefully as I could, I lifted them off with tape and fastened the strip to one of the evidence cards. I got right under the table lamp and compared them to what I had taken from the gun. No match that I could see.

The butter knife Billy Neal had played with came out of the napkin. You could see greasy fingerprints on it even without the dust. But I did get them sprinkled and lifted and taped to a card. The little booklet that came with my kit explained how to compare prints according to the Galton Pattern Type, which claims to be approved by the International Association for Criminal Identification. I guess that means it's for real. It uses a point system - twelve points of similarity equals identity - but I don't claim to have read the whole book. I was too tired and hungry at that moment to attempt to do so. But I can say that the prints Billy Neal left on that knife sure did look to my eye a lot like the ones I'd found on the barrel of the pistol that Allyn's boy had found on Siesta Key.

I had to wonder, if Neal was a murderer, why was his car still on Siesta Key hours after Higel's body had been found? Why had the gun been left behind, where the young man in the donkey-cart had happened to find it? Why would Billy Neal want to kill Harry Higel in the first place, and how was Noel A. Mitchell involved? He was Billy Neal's boss and supposedly Rube Allyn's friend, but how was that connected? Whoever killed Higel, how did he, or she, know that Mr. Higel would be walking down that sandy lane alone at 8 o'clock in the morning?

Something my boss, Burna Levi, said had stuck in my mind. "We don't need another botched investigation."

CHAPTER SEVENTEEN

A MURDERER IS REVEALED

Monday morning came up brisk and windy, meaning a storm was blowing around somewhere in the Gulf. Anyone who lives down here knows that feeling. Hot wind, cool wind, repeat. All the flowers blooming at once under a baking sun. Lizards scattering frantically. Tree tops waving back and forth. Birds racing around high in the sky, weaving this way and that – going somewhere. Then motionless air, until it's stirred up by yet another powerful gust.

I sat up in bed, realized that nothing had changed. I was still alone, and I still wasn't used to it. I cranked up a pot of coffee. I was still a First Deputy Sheriff who believed he had identified a possible murderer. That was one thing. Getting the powers-that-be lined up to do something about it was another thing. I fried some eggs and bologna and ate them out of the skillet. If Clarinda were here, we'd have plates. And biscuits. But what the hell.

I called around and learned that Sheriff Burna for some reason was out at Palmer Farms. I wanted to join him, but I had to gas up first thing and pulled into Harvey's Texaco on McIntosh Road, an old general store with an atmosphere I liked. Harvey's son, a red-headed kid with grease on his face and a New York Giants baseball cap tilted over his eyes, pumped my fuel and checked under the hood while I went inside.

"Howdy, Gabe," came from behind the cash register, where the proprietor was counting packs of Lucky Strikes. "Nineteen... twenty...."

"Sell many of those?" I asked. Packaged pre-rolled cigarettes were kind of a novelty item.

"Yessir, I do. Not as much as chaws and dip, but a lot of fellers like their smoke packaged up. How's the missus?"

He knew quite well Clarinda had gone somewhere. Every gossip around, and Harvey was first among them, knew that. I didn't enlighten him further and just shrugged.

Harvey has white hair and a yellow mustache, a round face and a gift for gab, which was sometimes enlightening or at least entertaining.

"What do you think about President Harding?" he asked, baiting me.

"Well, he's a Republican." Harvey knew I was a Democrat like just about everybody else was in Florida, but I had no particular dislike of the new man in the White House. I figured he couldn't be much worse than Woodrow Wilson, who got us into that terrible war.

"Think he'll do anything to stop them Bolsheviks?"

"You mean in Russia?"

"There, and here too!"

"I don't know a thing about that, Harvey. If you know any Bolsheviks around Bee Ridge, you sure better let me hear about it." I regretted saying that as soon as the words came out of my mouth. I meant it as a joke, but Harvey didn't take it that way at all. He had a sizeable list of known and potential Bolsheviks who should be watched in and around our community and the whole of Sarasota County, and he'd barely got started when I told him I'd have to be on my way. "But I'll be back," I assured him.

I gave the kid two bucks for the gas and told him to keep the change. Not much but it pleased him, and he gave my headlamps a wipe.

Sheriff Levi was in his old office at Palmer Farms fretting over reports of a wild bear attack on a hunter out by the head of the Myakka River, and the question was whether it had occurred in Sarasota or Manatee County. He had a map out and was on the phone to the Manatee County Sheriff. Burna thought it was out of his jurisdiction. Finally, it was agreed that he was correct, and the phone call ended.

"So," he exhaled. "What?"

I filled him in on my trip to St. Petersburg and meeting with Noel Mitchell. He started to grumble about something, but I told him about the threatening conversation with Billy Neal. Then I gave him the punch line about matching the finger prints.

"So, now you're a fingerprint expert," Burna said, skeptically.

"I'd say I'm the best you've got. At least I have an official kit and a book about it."

"Big deal. I don't think fingerprints are evidence."

"In some places they are," I argued. "But anyway, I believe this private detective, Billy Neal, held the gun which is in my possession by the barrel and used it as a club to kill Mayor Higel."

"Hmmm." The sheriff mulled it over. There it was. After a minute he smiled at the ceiling. "Deputy Bixby Hodges really screwed this up, didn't he? Pinning the crime on Rube Allyn," he said and looked pleased.

"I'm not so sure Rube is out of the picture, but I don't think he was the murderer."

"I don't really know what Bixby's game is," Burna went on. "It's taken me a few months to understand what's been going on in the City Marshal's office. What I've learned may or may not come as any surprise to you, Gabe."

"Anything you tell me will be news, since I don't know what Bixby has been up to all these years, but I guarantee it won't surprise me."

"He is making, this office has been making, something like $1,300 a month as its cut for leasing out city and county prisoners to the turpentine camps. It's been going into an account I wasn't aware of till now."

"I didn't know this office could get anything like that," I admitted. And I was impressed by the scale of the graft.

"The City Marshal has been getting paid for Sarasota prisoners. If he can place Manatee County prisoners, Bixby gets a cut of that. If he places a state prisoner in Sarasota County, he gets a piece of that. With me being elected, you'd think that would leave Bixby out. But, no. We've got our jail inmates working turpentine at five different camps in the county, all rented out before my time. The stills are continuing to pay something to someone for all that labor, but since my appointment, this sheriff hasn't seen one red cent."

"You think it's been going to Deputy Hodges?"

Burna spread out his arms. "I don't know for sure, Gabe. That's why I'm working out here on the Farm today. I don't know who to trust in my own Sheriff's office."

"Do you want me to get to work and straighten it out?" I asked. It was a job I'd enjoy.

"Probably," Burna said. "But first I've got to make my own phone calls and see who those camp managers think they're paying. And I'm wondering if some of these men's prison sentences haven't been served. In that case, they should be free to go about their business."

"If they survive. Have you been out to the camps, Burna?"

"No. Maybe I should go."

I nodded. "It's rough out there in the woods. Like slavery times, I suppose."

"I've never seen slavery," he said.

"Neither have I, but I imagine it's about like slashing pine trees in the hot sun all day while a white man on a horse watches you with his rifle."

"Don't get too sentimental on me, Gabe. But I get the picture. More pressing is this Higel case. You've got my attention, and my authority to push it forward. Get on back to Siesta Key and talk to Rube Allyn again. And to that boy who found the gun."

"Will do. I'll head out there right now."

"Good. Stop by City Hall. Take Bixby with you."

"Sir?"

"Rub it in, good, Gabe," he said, grinning like it was Christmas. "Rub it in."

I collected Deputy Hodges at the office. He was on the phone but hung up when he saw me come in. Bixby was keen to go as soon as I said I was driving out to the Key to interview Rube Allyn. It was almost like he was afraid of what Rube might say in private. Bixby wanted to be along, but said he preferred to go in his own car, so we drove over the new bridge, me in the lead.

It was windy crossing Sarasota Bay. Threatening black clouds blew across a hot white sky. We passed cars with fishing tackle strapped to their roofs coming back to the mainland. There was something dangerous in the air. I had the broken pistol, still loaded as it had been given to me, in a cigar box in my glove compartment, and for personal comfort I was wearing my Colt .45 Government Model. I had started using it for business purposes when I retired the old 1870's Peacemaker I'd inherited from my father. That heirloom went into a strongbox at home. Mack coveted it, but he'd have to wait awhile. My new pistol didn't weigh a whole lot less than the old one – you needed a tight holster strap for both of them - but it looked more professional than my old six-shooter. So I was powerfully and legally armed, which was comforting because whenever you're around armed men and investigating a murder you're in a risky business.

With Bixby trailing, I drove right past the turn-off onto Higel Avenue. I didn't want to bother the widow by crossing over her property to reach the Bayou Louise bridge. Instead I continued on to Gulfmead Drive and made my right, passing again the parade of "lots for sale" signs - but now one new house was actually under construction - before I reached the Allyn place at the end of the beach road. Shells had been spread over the roadway since last

I was there, making for much better traction than packed sand. I could hear Bixby Hodges' police Ford crunching along behind me.

It was a lonely spot on an overcast day. Rube Allyn's house looked to be abandoned. The porch furniture was gone and the windows were shuttered, but Allyn's car was there. And by the time I parked and got out to stretch, Rube had stepped out onto his porch to see who these intruders were. He watched as Deputy Bixby Hodges pulled in beside me.

"What's all this about?" he shouted. His hair was whipping around.

"Just a talk, Rube," I yelled back.

"Then what's he doing here?" He pointed at Deputy Bixby.

I wasn't too sure myself, but I called out, "Maybe he wants to apologize for arresting you."

"Not likely," Hodges grunted. "I'm here to see justice is done!" he bellowed, "but we don't have any warrant for you, if that's what you're asking."

"We can talk from here," Rube said.

"No, that won't do, Rube," I said. "Don't make this any more complicated than it has to be. I think you can be of help to me in my investigation of some new evidence. We got to come inside and speak. I can barely hear you out here." I walked to the porch stairs and continued up.

Rube didn't try to block my way, so I stepped around him and went through his front door. The place was almost completely bare. All of the furniture, the books, rugs, lamps, pictures, everything, was gone. The only things left that I could see were a kitchen table with a box of Toasted Corn Flakes on it, some dirty dishes, and two wooden chairs. One of them was occupied by Rube's son Lewellen, the one who had given me the gun. A pair of crutches leaned against the table beside him. The place was dim, with most of the shutters closed. Just one window in the room was open to let in the air and some sunlight. I don't think they had any electricity for lights. Wind gusts were making quite a noise, whipping through the palms and rattling the house.

Bixby Hodges brushed by Rube and came in, too. He took in the scene and shook his head like it was just as desolate as he would expect. Reluctantly, Rube followed us into his own house. He didn't close the door behind him. That was good. I don't like being so confined with pissed off people.

The young man, Lewellen, said, "Hello." At least he was friendly.

"Hello, yourself," I said. "Remember me?"

"Sure." He squinted his eyes like we shared a secret.

"You gave me the pistol you found."

He frowned. I had let his secret out. "Maybe," he said cautiously.

"No 'maybe' about it." I turned my attention to Rube and filled him in on receiving the gun. I asked him what he knew about it.

"Not a thing!" he insisted. "And I can hardly believe Lewellen found such weaponry and never even told me." He glowered at his son, who bowed his head.

"Looks like you're almost finished with your packing," I observed. Bixby was roaming around the room, looking for incriminating evidence I surmised. He picked up the Corn Flakes box and looked inside. Apparently it contained Corn Flakes. He set it down.

"My family has moved on," Rube explained. "I'm just down here taking care of a few of my final affairs. I had planned to spend the week here, but the weather seems stormy. We might depart tonight. Thanks to that man," he flicked a finger at Hodges without even looking at him, "I have no wish to remain in Sarasota, or to ever see it again." He tossed his hair back and gave me his full square-jaw expression.

I turned to his son. "Do you remember finding the pistol?" I asked. He nodded. "Where?"

"Down the road, in the bushes," he mumbled. "In the bushes. I could take you there."

"That's what I want you to do. I still have that gun, you know? And guess what else I've discovered?"

He cocked his head.

"I believe it belongs to a man in St. Petersburg named Billy Neal."

Both Rube and Bixby perked up their ears at this.

"That's right," I went on, now addressing the two men. "I went up to St. Petersburg and talked to this Billy Neal and to his boss, Noel Mitchell. Know them, do you?" I asked Rube. He was shaking in indignation, a wounded entertainer.

"Noel is a dear friend! I've never heard of this Billy what's-his-name!" He stood poised and hard as a statue.

I raised my voice. "Billy what's-his-name was right here on the Key when Harry Higel was killed," I pressed on. "Why was he here? If he beat Higel to death, why did he do it? Why did he lose the murder weapon in the bushes? Why was Noel Mitchell's man, your friend's sharpshooter detective, here, right down the road from your house, on that morning? Tell me!" I stepped toward him, holding his eyes.

"Hey, wait a minute," Bixby said behind me, interfering.

"Ask him! Ask Bixby!" Rube yelled and pointed a long forefinger at the deputy. "He's the one set the whole thing up!"

I was too surprised by the suddenness of that accusation to react as quickly as I should have. Before I could swing around and draw down on my fellow law enforcer, Bixby had his own gun pointed at me. And the room was shadowed by another player.

"Now, that ain't polite," Billy Neal said from the doorway. He had a big pistol, too, pointed at everyone but especially me. And he wasn't grinning.

"The murderer reveals himself," I announced, as if I were some master sleuth instead of a country lawman who just got caught flatfooted by a hood.

"Who in blazes is this man?" Rube yelled. "I want you all out of my house!" His son was staring wildly from person to person. He clutched his crutches against his chest.

"Not likely," Neal said, advancing into the room.

Rube turned on Deputy Bixby. "You brought all of this down on me!" he shouted. "Now everyone in town thinks I'm a murderer! And sixty-one days in jail! My God! Sixty-one days in jail!"

"Wait!" My hands were in the air. "What did Harry Higel ever do to any of you?"

Bixby walked right up to me where I could feel and smell his breath, "For starters," he said, "Higel was going to finance the campaign of D.R. Brown to run against me for Sheriff as soon as Burna Levi's term is up – just as soon as Burna gets out of my way."

Bixby telling me this let me know I was personally no longer in his future plans. Between him and Billy Neal, I was planning to be dead. But, to keep him talking...

"What's so great about being sheriff?" I asked him. "The job doesn't pay very much."

Rube provided the answer. "The prisoner camps!" he shouted, scarlet face ablaze. "These scoundrels make their money off of the turpentine camps, the blood of the poor savages!"

"Yeah?" I looked around. "So how'd you get involved, Rube?"

"Leave it!" Billy Neal ordered.

"I won't leave it," Rube objected. "Harry Higel was the worst neighbor a man could have. He fenced off our bridge over the bayou. He pestered me, all the time, about a mortgage he claimed I owed him. Knowing full well that I was and am in dire straits with six mouths to feed. Knowing full well that printing a newspaper is an intellectual vocation, not a profit-making enterprise. And my son, my dear Lewellen...," he pointed to the young man who was watching us all, wide-eyed, "...Just because on occasion this young man left open a chicken pen and let a few of His Majesty Higel's brave cocks roam free, they banned him from their property. And they hated his poor donkey, whom they complained brayed in the morning, like all donkeys do, and he defecated in the roadway while pulling Lewellen about. Oh, the privileged Higels, as if the streets somehow belonged to them. Lord Harry blocked the bayou bridge so I couldn't drive across it. There were many, many reasons I wished Harry Higel gone. But did I kill him? No!"

Exhausted by that, he sat down in the other chair. And wiped his brow! Now it was just the three of us standing. Billy Neal had a pistol pointed at me, and Bixby had another one. Bixby ran his fingers though his hair wondering how to pull this off, then he holstered his gun.

"I didn't like the man, Harry Higel," Rube said quietly from his chair, ignoring the rest of us. "I admit that. No secret. And I mentioned my dislike to Noel Mitchell. Just mentioned it. We often talk and socialize. Then this man," again he pointed a stern finger at Bixby Hodges, "came out here to answer one of my numerous complaints about Higel's annoying behavior. I was pretty hot about it, and I said more than I should have. I gave the deputy the whole list of the lousy things Higel had done to me. This so-called stalwart of the law," he said scornfully to Bixby, "made no bones about his own dislike of Higel. And, yes, I may have disclosed to this so-called deputy sheriff my close friendship with Noel Mitchell, the mayor of St. Petersburg, and the fact that he didn't care for Harry Higel either. Higel was competing with Noel in the ocean-front real estate business. I may have mentioned to Bixby that Noel had a detective agency which was famous for 'taking care of things.' I sent that idea aloft, a seed that might fall to earth, plant itself and grow. Bixby could carry that information on from there, wherever he thought best. But I never imagined . . ." Rube wound down. He stared at his clasped hands.

"You're such a bullshitter," Bixby Hodges told Rube.

"In spades," Billy Neal said.

"What are you saying, Rube?" I protested. "You never imagined that Noel Mitchell and Bixby Hodges would conspire to, what...?" but I was cut off.

"I'll take that gun," Bixby said, addressing me. He got in close and lifted my service weapon. He handed it to Billy Neal, who checked to see that it was loaded.

Billy Neal then did a curious thing. He crouched, watching me the whole time, and laid my gun on the floor between his boots.

The scene was set. Bixby asked Billy Neal, "Have you got this under control?"

"Oh, yeah," Neal responded, keeping me covered.

"Then I'm gone. Bye, Gabe." And Bixby walked out the door. I didn't hear his car start any more than I had heard Billy Neal's car drive up. The whistling wind was drowning out most everything. I looked around the room. It seemed to be shaking from the gale. Or was I? The Allyns, Rube and son, turned their eyes away. Billy Neal smiled at me. "Want your gun?" he asked.

CHAPTER EIGHTEEN

THE MURDERER IS PUNISHED

Rube's son broke the spell in the emptied room. "Papa didn't do anything wrong!" he cried.

"That's right!" his father said emphatically. "That's one hundred percent right!"

"You hear that, Billy?" I asked the man with all the guns. "You drove down here and figured out how to kill Harry Higel all by yourself? Rube had nothing to do with it? You sure are a smart murderer, Billy. Why did you make such a messy job of it?"

"Yes I drove here," Billy Neal said, keeping a mean eye on me and a steady hand on his pistol, "but, Rube. . ." - he looked through me to Allyn - "don't you remember meeting me on the beach road? And telling me that Higel would be coming down the lane, taking his morning constitutional, any minute. And didn't you tell me right where he'd be? How about it, Rube?"

Rube puffed his cheeks and exhaled mightily. "You said you would talk to him, scare him, threaten him. Not beat him to a pulp!"

"No, I said I would shoot the son of a bitch, and you said 'I don't care what you do.' And I would have done just that, but for the dumb colored carpenter who showed up right when I had Higel in my sights. And they talked and talked. And as soon as that fool went on his way your idiot boy here rolls by in his stupid donkey cart. What was that about Rube? Couldn't you keep your boy at home? Did you want me to pin the job on your boy? He'd get off for being retarded, wouldn't he? It might look like an accident, if the gun was his."

"I don't know what you're talking about!" Rube yelled. Lewellen's head was still bowed, facing the table top. "My son doesn't even own any gun!"

"You don't need to own a gun," Neal said, reasoning it out. Reasoning how he was being framed. Or how Rube had planned to frame his son. "You just need to be caught with one in your hands. But your boy, I saw him, he took one look at Higel and rode away. Higel turned around to go back to his house, and the colored man wasn't far off yet, and there was no way I could shoot, was there? Everybody would hear."

I spoke up and took a step in his direction. "And that's when you scrambled out of the bushes and beat him to death, right, Billy?" I took another step, but he raised the pistol to level with my chin, and I decided to stand as steady as I could.

"Yes, I beat his head in!" Neal yelled. "I smacked him before he knew it was coming. My job was to see him dead, but before I could finish the job proper, up comes a pick-up truck, and those boys spotted the body. I had to move quick to get out of there."

"Back to where you left your car." I said.

"That's right, dead man. But I was stuck, wasn't I? I knew I couldn't get back to the bridge with all the commotion going on. I had to lay low. Couldn't go to the beach." Neal had a crazy smile on his face, explaining how smart he was. Rushing it, he said, "There were some guys there surf fishing. I heard the sirens coming. And then just when it quiets down and I'm suffering from being out of butts, you come walking by. You sniff around my car. And then this damn dummy boy rides up again, and you and he have a long talk. I might have planted the gun on the boy but for you showing up. I was thinking about plugging you both just to get out of the heat. Finally, you turned around and walked back toward Higel's house, and I made a run for it."

"And the gun?" I was sweating, but I asked anyway, looking for some way out.

"I tossed that away," Billy said with a crooked grin. "Didn't want to be caught with it, for sure. It was broken anyway. And bloody."

He took a deep breath after all that talking and put his boot heel on my revolver.

"How about you kill this rat?" he calmly asked Rube Allyn, who was sitting silently off-stage. "And let's be done with it. You started this, didn't you?" Neal's face had gone from white to red and now, seemed to me, had turned to something like yellow. I had no doubt he was about to blow my head off.

The abrupt question brought Rube back to his feet.

"I am no killer!" the thespian proclaimed. Had it not been for my sincere respect for Billy Neal's murderous nature, I would have thought

I was in the middle of a theatrical performance at a vaudeville house. "To think you intended to implicate my son!" Rube went on. "You dog! You dog, sir! And I deny what you say! I woke up early that morning, that's true. Even after my long drive home from St. Petersburg. I got out of bed and came looking for you. In some moment over a bottle of red wine with Noel, I must have heard that you would be here and I must have agreed to guide you. It's all foggy in my memory. I lacked sleep. I walked the beach in search of you, I did, but instead of finding you I found Harry's lifeless body. One look and I knew I was too late to help him. Of course I ran! Who wouldn't? Back to my own house. I swam the bayou in my panic to avoid being seen. But to say I'm a killer, like you? That's absurd!"

Billy Neal laughed at him. "I'd work on that story, if I was you, Rube. Maybe Noel could help you write it up just like that, for the papers. But I ain't taking a chance." He stooped suddenly and snatched up my revolver with his free hand. Now he had a pistol in both fists. "You're going the same place as this Deputy Sheriff MacFarlane is going".

"Papa, No!" the young man, Lewellyn, screamed and turned over the table. Billy Neal fired his gun at something, I didn't wait around to find out what he hit. I leapt for the one window whose shutters had been left open and fell about ten feet down to the sand. I don't know if it hurt or not, I just kept going, running for the palmettos. Scrambling into the brush, I think I realized something was painful, but I was crawling for my life.

Shots were being fired, at me, as I expected, but what I had in mind was circling around through the undergrowth and making a run for my car. If I couldn't drive it, maybe I could get that still-loaded murder weapon out of the cigar box in my glove compartment.

Some sort of tussle must have been going on inside the Allyn house to take the attention off me momentarily because I managed to wriggle on my knees and elbows back to the Dodge and pry open the door. I got the box, and the pistol.

Billy Neal ran out on the porch and fired down at me. Me, running back in the woods now, dashing from tree to tree, dodging bullets, I heard Neal banging down the steps and coming in pursuit, crashing through the scrub.

I reached the beach, but needing a place to catch my breath, I stayed close against the trees and staggered southward. I calculated I still had the six rounds in the Police Positive's cylinder, but the firing mechanism might not work with all the pounding the gun had taken against Higel's skull.

The storm that had been threatening all day started in earnest now. Wind was raking the sand, lifting up sudden sheets of it and flinging them like blankets into the palm line. Sea foam blew up in twisters that danced into the dunes. I stayed close to the bending palms and scrub grass, looking for a log to get behind.

I spied a broken cedar tree's stump a few feet back into the woods. Small cover but I went for it and stuck my boot a foot deep into a gopher tortoise hole. That tripped me up good, and something in my ankle broke or got a powerful twist. I was down in the sand and palmetto spears, and I had to bite my lower lip to keep from screaming in pain. Then here comes Billy Neal stalking like a night owl through the brush, barely visible under the low green branches, right after me. He was silhouetted for a moment perfectly by the brilliant sun descending to the horizon behind him. There were jet-black clouds towering above his head. I remember that. The wind had torn away his hat. I shot him right in the middle of his chest. And he went down.

Down with me, onto the rough sunbaked ground, with the beetles and the lizards and the little crabs, gasping for breath. As was I, sucking air through my mouth, careless of gnats and the sweat flowing down my face. I was breathing and Billy Neal wasn't.

Time passed, and I managed to get back to my feet. I kicked Neal over, and he was clearly dead. His face wasn't any prettier dead than when he was alive. I didn't like looking at it, so I rolled him back over on his belly and dragged him a few feet deeper into the wood.

I had one good leg. The other was a challenge but not broken, evidently, because I could limp. Billy Neal had been shooting at me with my own single-action, which I reclaimed and put back in its holster on my belt. The Higel murder weapon, the one I'd shot Billy with - to be truthful

I was just too tired to know what to do with it - so I dropped it beside Billy's corpse. I'd be back and collect all this mess, I thought. First, I needed to hike back to the Allyn house to see what damage Billy Neal had done to the people there.

I hobbled back to the public lane, dragging my bad leg the whole way. The roadbed was hard sand and shells, but no cars or people appeared to help me along. I'd never seen too many tourists, construction workers, or islanders out on the Key, despite all the "Land For Sale" signs, and on this blustery afternoon there were none whatsoever. The wind was up and quick showers of rain blasted by.

The Allyn place, at land's end, was just as deserted as everything else. Rube's car was gone. I limped up the porch steps, one at the time, and barreled through the front door with my shoulder. The house was empty. Rube and his son, Lewellen, had departed. Even the table and chairs were gone, amazing composure on their part. The only sign of recent habitation was the squashed Corn Flakes box on the floor.

The shutters were slamming back and forth against the window I had exited through. I pulled them closed and fastened the latch. In light of the coming storm, I was being a good neighbor, I guess.

Back on the porch, sitting down on the top step, I could listen to the mounting gale and collect my thoughts. What kind of story, I wondered, did the good Deputy Bixby Hodges plan to tell to explain my disappearance – the disappearance he was counting on? He must be telling Burna something. My unexplained failure to return. Surely, no mishap? About how I might be dead.

Bixby would eventually come searching for me. He would expect to find my dead body, felled by my own gun. For that story to work, he'd have to count on Rube and his son keeping silent about the whole affair. Since it seemed like Rube was as much to blame as Billy Neal for the Higel killing, that was good bet, I'd say. But, Bixby would be worried about what other mayhem Billy Neal might have accomplished in those moments before he came for me. He might have killed not just me but the Allyns, too. Bixby wouldn't know until he came back. If he found them dead, they would probably have been killed with my gun. Billy Neal was careful and would have seen to that detail. Bixby wouldn't know who all was dead, until he came back to see, after I was reported missing. If all three of us, the Allyns and me, had been killed with my gun, Bixby would have to come up with a way to spin that yarn. Some way or another. Once he came back to investigate, which could be soon.

That thought got me moving. I'd had enough of gunplay for one day, where I was the target. With the wind at my back and pushing me along, I found myself behind the wheel, and I drove as fast as I could toward the bridge.

Rolling into Sarasota I thought about what I would say to Bixby after I surprised him by being alive. And what I would say to my boss, Burna. I'd tell how it happened, but of course Bixby would deny everything. He would say he left me, in good health, on Siesta Key after we both interviewed Rube Allyn. Bixby would swear that nothing had come out during the interview, so he came home. Deputy MacFarlane had stayed behind because he wanted to sightsee, or whatever. Bixby would show his distaste for me and my methods when he said that. He would deny knowing anything about anyone named Billy Neal or where Rube Allyn might be. Unless Rube's body was on the floor. In which case, there's be no one to blame but me. My motive? "I'm not a genius, boss," Bixby would say. "Just an honest cop."

I'd call Bixby a liar and take Burna out to see the body of Billy Neal. Who I had killed, with the gun I claimed he had used to kill Harry Higel. But I'd used that gun to kill Billy after he had shot at me, not with his own pistol but with mine. The very pistol I had now in my own holster. But it wouldn't sound right that Billy Neal was shooting at me with my own gun. Who would back me up on any of that? Rube Allyn? These arrows were all pointing at me, guilty Gawain MacFarlane.

So I did not drive to the Sheriff's office. I was wind-blown, cut up, shot at, gopher-tortoised, tired, and screwed, and I kept my old Dodge rolling straight to the front yard of my empty house. Where the intensifying storm was blowing the pine trees and sweeping the sand off the grass and up onto my porch. The door slammed behind me all by itself, and I went to a bottom shelf where I knew there was an old bottle of whiskey I'd been saving for a special occasion. Having killed my first man after thirty-five years of wearing a badge, this was the occasion.

I went to bed, my lonely cot.

And that's when it flooded back. Ghosts. Ghosts of the cannibal,

Zechariah, in the Blackjack, and the words he spoke there. "You have to believe. How can you live otherwise?" Believe Gawain! It must mean something to kill a man. You wake up and know, still, you've done that. That's something to explain to Peter. Good Lord, Gawain, get it together! It happened! Press it into your heart!

I took deep breaths.

A storm raged outside. I slept.

CHAPTER NINETEEN
A HURRICANE WITH NO NAME

I woke up late the next morning, startled by a water bucket, one I had carelessly dropped in my yard, flattening itself against my front door. The sound was like a hammer smashing against an anvil, and I instantly became alert. Then my ears received the whole drum and bugle corps of nature, as waves of rain, tree branches, and probably squirrels and possums flew at the walls of my house. I stumbled out of bed and pushed open the front door, just enough to get a blast of the Gulf of Mexico in my face, and that discouraged me from any further investigation. The joints of the building creaked, and the roof sounded like God was pouring lard cans of marbles right over me and all the inhabitants of Catfish Creek. My old place shook, but it held together.

It took all day for the storm to pass, and I had little to do except pace the floor anxiously and try to calm my dog, who forgot everything he ever knew about indoor sanitation. I cleaned my guns. I read the Bible. I played my guitar and sang some old songs. Finally, by late afternoon, the rain settled down to something approaching normal and I could venture outside. Even the sun broke through.

My citrus groves were a mess. Before the storm, my oranges and grapefruit had just started to ripen abundantly, but now their fruit had fallen like a carpet onto the mud. My barn doors had blown wide open, and a lot of hay had gotten wet. Luckily, I had taken to boarding my horse, Pardner, at a stall on Palmer Farms, which, being a few miles inland, may have saved his life.

My new Dodge started up, but there was no place for a car to go. Tree limbs covered my driveway and everything else. I was gimping on one leg, but I went to work getting the obstacles cleared away. It took some hours to finish that. Then I went to check on my neighbors. They were all doing the same thing, and, as it was in our power, we all helped straighten out our little community. The pastor at our Oak Grove Church called a prayer meeting and dinner on the church grounds for that evening, and people brought lots of covered dishes, which we ate by lantern light. It was a good time for us all, who felt like survivors of Noah's flood.

It was the next morning before I could drive back to Sarasota. A lot had changed, and was changing. A chain of people was dragging muddy furniture out of City Hall so that it could dry. The end of Main Street was impassable because the Seaboard Airline tracks that ran out to the pier had been ripped up and bent shoreward by the storm. Mangled bands of twisted steel had been driven through the seawall and flung across Gulfstream Avenue. Quite a tribute to the power of Mother Nature. Almost all of the warehouses, machine shops and fish houses along the Bayfront had been reduced to piles of rubble. Boats, big and small, were half-sunk and adrift in the sea water or had been thrown ashore. Electric poles were scattered on the ground like match sticks. People I knew, and many I didn't, were wandering about, surveying the damage, and telling each other their stories. But instead of doing my job and helping to restore law and order, I got back in my car and rode off in search of Billy Neal's corpse.

The bridge over Sarasota Bay was intact, but the roadway was covered with piles of sand, palm fronds, fish and shells. I managed to drive through the clutter, some of which was still flopping and wriggling, just hoping I could eventually make it back again.

Siesta Key in its entirety was unrecognizable. A tidal surge had raked the whole island. To cause such destruction it must have been at least seven feet high when it came ashore. The trees were snapped or doubled over – not just the planted trees but also the mangrove forests - were flattened and bent, and what had been streets were basically buried in mounds of sand. I drove as far as Higel Avenue, where the savagely beaten body of poor Harry Higel had been found. Beyond that point, the roadway had been scoured away to oblivion and totally buried by the drifts. There was nothing to do but park and continue on foot. And that wasn't so easy with my bum leg, but who's complaining?

It was hot. Sand was piled over the sea oats and halfway up the palm trees. The pines and palmettos were stripped of all their green, making our once-tropical paradise look like pictures you may have seen of the Sahara Desert. If you subscribed to the National Geographic, as we did. Emerging onto the beach, the terrible images of devastation vanished, replaced by the calm, blue sea, as beautiful and unaffected as it had been since creation. Gentle waves rolled in and out. White birds soared in their simple patterns. The breezes smelled of sweet, foreign salts. But I had left Billy Neal's body somewhere nearby and I needed to find it.

I limped into the woods and searched for that body. But it wasn't where I thought it should be. On my knees, pulling away pieces of trees and piles of seaweed from the sand I became increasingly desperate. I crashed about, overturning fallen limbs, digging in the dirt, kicking away what was left of uprooted bushes.

Neal was not where I thought I'd plugged him, unless he was buried deep in the dunes. The broken pistol I'd shot him with was gone. Hell, so was the stump I'd taken cover behind. Even the gopher tortoise hole was filled in.

I had to wonder if someone had removed the body. Or had it just washed away? My hope was that the sea had taken it. Or was it interred below me in the sand? More than he deserved.

Beautiful as the seascape now was, there was no use for me being there, no corpse to report. Nothing left to explain about what I had been through. It would have to be my story, to keep inside.

So I drove back to Sarasota, propelled by heavy winds, to make my report to Sheriff Levi, and to learn whether Bixby had reported me dead. And to receive my orders.

The sheriff's office was open, but the only officer present was Investigator Brown, the dog-handler. Bixby was worried that this man was going to run against him in the next election, so despite his incompetence I wished him well.

"Sheriff and Deputy Hodges are out at the McKeithan turpentine camp," Brown told me. "The hurricane blew the place out, and there's been some killings."

I drove to the Laurel camp, miles away, as fast as I could. Considering that the road conditions weren't the best, it took two hours, and I saw lots of misery along that route. Houses had been flattened, and people, stranded beside the highway, were begging for food, or clothes, or help of any kind. Trees were toppled, right and left.

The gate to the camp was open. Even approaching from a distance you could smell the acrid smoke. I found the sheriff's car parked among several others outside the smoldering remains of the bunkhouses and the camp kitchen. The stockade fences were flattened to the ground. Black men, about a dozen of them, were huddled in a cluster on the encampment's charred ashen dirt, ankles and wrists shackled together. They dropped their heads and avoided looking my way. I got out of the car and walked as fast as I could further down the dirt road to where the turpentine still had stood by the railroad spur. But the still, the mainstay of the operation, had been reduced to a hot pile of burning timbers in an acre of scorched earth and blackened loblolly pines. Several men were gathered there, studying the debris. Among them I saw Sheriff Levi, Deputy Bixby Hodges, the camp's manager McFeed, and a smattering of others. The Woodsrider was not among therm. I joined their circle, nodding around at the troubled faces. Bixby Hodges jerked up straight, surprised to see me alive. The camp manager, McFeed, his soot-covered face streaked with sweat under a stained limp hat, was excitedly describing a night of horrors.

"The wind came in right after midnight," he said, gesturing with his hands like he was the wind, "and the men set up such a howl, screaming to be let out. The building was shaking." McFee shook as a demonstration. "Then a tree blew over on the roof and somehow that busted the door locks. I came running with my trustees, but them prisoners got a gun someways and started firing back. Then they went running all over the camp, tearing off into the woods. My guards chased after them, but it was pitch black and branches were flying everywhere. Then the still caught fire. I don't know if them prisoners did it or it was a lightning strike. Not a thing we could do about it then!" He was tired and pleading for understanding. "It was raining cats and dogs, but the turpentine, all those barrels, just exploded in the flames, flared up into the pine trees. The wind spread the fire throughout the camp. So we just hunkered down till dawn and watched it all go." McFeed took a few deep breaths.

"As soon as I could see my hand in front of my face," he continued, "we rode back into the woods to collect what prisoners we could find. The Woodsrider was up in front on his horse, flushing them out of the bushes. Then the shooting started again. I don't know how many he killed or wounded. He was way off in the trees. I came upon dead man after dead man, but I couldn't catch up to him. But, eventually. . . I found Leather Britches. Laying up against a tree, his head split open with an axe, to where you could see his . . . brains, and his horse was gone. And the axe, too." McFeed paused for air. "We rounded up what few prisoners we found alive. That's them you saw over by the camp. I don't know how many escaped or how many is laying out there in the woods. Might we say the storm killed them?" he suggested.

"You wasted a lot of good manpower, seems to me," Deputy Hodges said angrily.

"I know you can find us some more, Bixby, can't you?" The camp manager's tone was almost accusing.

"Don't talk that way to me!" Hodges said quietly. "Wouldn't surprise me one bit if you had twenty of them prisoners hidden where they can be your slaves without you having to pay anything for their services."

"You men just shut up!" Sheriff Levi ordered. "Bixby, you're going to stay down here and do an inventory of every man, dead, alive or missing. Be very thorough about it. We'll need to explain what became of each one of them. Their kin will want to know. And y'all see that any of them bodies that don't get claimed gets buried. As for this Woodsrider, collect his personal belongings, if there are any, and bring them back to Sarasota. His family may want them. And no doubt they'll want whoever killed him brought to trial."

Bixby Hodges chewed his lip, but I think he agreed with the job, since he'd want to know where his business stood.

"MacFarlane, you follow me back to town." With that Burna turned away and plodded back toward his car. Bixby put a hand on my shoulder, which I knocked off.

"I don't know how you managed to stay alive," he growled at me. "I advise you to be very careful what you say about anything you may think you heard about Harry Higel's murder. Unless, of course, you can prove something, which you can't. I'll be watching my back around you MacFarlane."

"Don't worry about your back, Bixby," I told him. "When I come for you it'll be right in your face."

But as I hiked back to my car I had to admit that he'd made a good point about lack of proof.

The turpentine camp got up and running before Thanksgiving. Bixby found some more convicts in DeSoto County that he could arrange to rent out, and they rebuilt it. Bixby did prepare the inventory that Sheriff Levi had requested. I happened to be in the office when he came in. I ignored him as usual. He tossed his paperwork on the secretary's desk to be typed up, glared at me, and went back outside, probably to find a free meal. The secretary got a start on it, but lunchtime rolled around and she had a date with a sailor, so she said. Naturally I picked up Bixby's hand-printed list and sat down to read it.

The name "Seth Ephram" appeared with the notation "Escaped and Wanted." It was the easiest thing in the world to get a pencil from her desk, erase those words and replace them with "Dead and Buried."

In a day or two I took a ride out to where his dad, Jake, lived and gave him the news.

"Seth ain't dead. He's stowed out in the barn," the man confessed.

"I guess the records must be mistaken, then," I said. "So what's Seth got? About one month left on his original sentence? And the judge can tack on five more years for escaping."

We stood quietly for a minute.

"How'd your oranges do in the storm?" I asked finally.

"Unless they were already boxed up, they hit the ground. All you can do is gather 'em up, clean 'em off, and sell them for juice. Got to move quick though," he replied.

"You could always go and correct the record of Seth's death, Jake. Or

Seth could turn himself in and take his chances."

Jake Ephram took a long time to think this over. The jaw worked in his normally frowning face. "The deck is always stacked, ain't it?" he said finally. His expression became hard and grim.

"Or Seth could leave from around here and start over in a new place," I suggested.

"He's got an aunt in Chicago," Jake said thoughtfully.

"And a girlfriend in Osprey. Maybe she'd like to travel."

"Well," Jake said, meaning the conversation was over.

In my pants pocket were five rolled-up Ben Franklins. I'd brought them to this meeting, not sure whether I'd hand them over. But I did, and Jake took the money.

Jake's mother, Missus Cordelia, had told me when I was a young boy not to be "jaundiced," by which she meant don't act like I assume all those powerful people are bad. But I am jaundiced, and they are bad. Helping her grandson escape to a new life was one thing I could do to balance the scales — not much, but some.

CHAPTER TWENTY

RETIREMENT

Nobody ever came around the office to ask about Billy Neal, the marksman from St. Pete. I don't know if that was because he didn't have a family, or because nobody cared for him enough to inquire about his disappearance. Nor was there a peep from his boss, Noel A. Mitchell, the Mayor of St. Petersburg and head of a "national" detective agency. I guess he had lost interest in "detecting" this murder.

It made me happy to learn that Mitchell had problems of his own. Having got himself elected mayor of St. Pete by courting the women's vote, which had just then come into existence, he seemed to have forgotten that a whole lot of those particular voters were passionately against drinking.

Notwithstanding Prohibition, Mitchell himself did believe in drinking. He not only drank socially, he partied lavishly, and unfortunately for him, he had the bad judgment to host those parties in the Mayor's office. In November one of these festivities got raided by the police, apparently not his base of support, and not only was the merry-making broken up but the mayor himself was arrested for public drunkenness. He protested, and Rube Allyn's paper carried a full-page statement proclaiming his innocence. Nevertheless, there was a quick recall election, and Noel A. Mitchell was tossed out.

Back home in Sarasota, Burna Levi was approaching the end of his tenure as our new county's first sheriff. He said he no longer wanted the job. More accurately, the Palmers were satisfied with the way Sarasota was headed and didn't feel the need to have their own handpicked sheriff anymore. Before Burna left he came up with a plan for the reorganization of the Sheriff's department. In his plan, under the sheriff would be a Chief Deputy, a Traffic Officer, a Head of Road Gang, and two or more regular Deputies to help with the ordinary business, which was becoming: Break Up The Stills! The Volstead Act was the law of the land now!

Burna assured me that the Chief Deputy's job belonged to me, but that was just pie in the sky. Any new sheriff coming in, given who the likely candidates were, would fire me in a minute. So, I continued my work, policing the streets and being sure my reports were turned in on time, until the election.

In December of 1921 Bixby Hodges was selected by the voters to be the second sheriff of Sarasota County, almost without opposition. The competition he feared from Investigator D.R. Brown, the man who was supposed to be Harry Higel's candidate, never materialized. The day Hodges took office I handed in my resignation. We exchanged insults, spoken quietly so the staff wouldn't hear. I gave him a one-finger salute and tossed my badge on his desk. In a week, he had filled all the jobs that Burna had envisioned, and thus built up quite a staff of law enforcers.

As sheriff, Bixby Hodges finally had free rein with the convict leasing business. Anyone he arrested, he could lease out. Any prisoners from other counties whom he could place in one of the private prison camps in Sarasota County, he got a piece of.

But, guess what! Some poor vagrant from North Dakota named Martin Tabert got busted riding the rails (what they called "being on a train without a ticket") in Tallahassee. He was convicted and told to pay a $25 fine which he didn't have at the moment. Although his parents wired the fine, plus another $25 to pay for a ticket home, the money disappeared into the Leon County prison system. The same could have happened in Sarasota County, I can attest.

The boy, and that's what he was, was leased out to the Putnam Lumber Company in Clara, which is up in Dixie County somewhere above the Steinhatchee River. I've never been there, but I read about the case. Young Martin got crosswise with the "whipping boss," the newspapers said, who flogged him to death. They printed the boss's name, Thomas Walter Higginbotham, in papers all the way to New York City.

The whole calamity – since it happened to a white boy – became so embarrassing, even to the point of discouraging tourism and real estate investment, that Governor Hardee issued an order ending convict labor in the entire state of Florida. That governor did a number of other things they called "progressive," such as getting rid of the state income tax and ruling in electrocution to replace hanging for our convicted murderers. But the one about convict labor did in Bixby Hodges. Losing convict lease payments was big. There was only so much money to be made protecting bootleggers.

After his second term, Bixby was opposed by his own Road Gang Deputy, W.D. Keen, and got voted out of office.

CHAPTER TWENTY-ONE

THE SARASOTA CELERY FIELDS

Rube Allyn, bless his heart, moved north of Tampa to recover from his association with Harry Higel's murder. He started publishing a sportsman's magazine. It was called Florida Fisherman, and it was popular I think, though I never bought it. His family carried it on. I'm told his kids all turned out well.

It took some time, but Sarasota got cleaned up from that October 1921 hurricane. The City powers took advantage of the destruction along the Bayfront to buy the whole of it and decree that the waterside would henceforth be for recreational and tourism purposes only. They built a new Municipal Pier, out of concrete this time, and banned all fish houses, machine shops and warehouses from the area. Majestic royal palms were planted where fish nets had been, and we became a beautiful city in competition with St. Petersburg and the other tourist draws of the Sunshine State. It was hard to believe that ten years earlier hogs and cattle had been allowed to roam and graze freely about our Sarasota city streets.

After I quit the Sheriff's office, I went straight back to work at Palmer Farms as Security Manager. With Clarinda gone, there was no one waiting for me at home so why wouldn't I want to keep working? Clarinda was orbiting somewhere on her own planet. I was going slightly nuts all by myself.

The Palmers' biggest operation, next to real estate development, was no longer their cattle ranches but the Celery Fields. Miles and miles of land - from Fruitville Road all the way to Bee Ridge and a new thoroughfare they named Palmer Avenue - had been leveled, filled, ditched, irrigated and set out to produce the finest celery sold anywhere in the world.

It was billed as "Muck-Grown Celery," and that's because the newly cultivated soil was bog-like, which means that when you walked between the rows your shoes sunk into the mud. All of that land used to be swampy wetland. But the Palmers had led the way to drain about 26,000 acres, which is forty square miles, and to build fifty miles of canals to make this agriculture happen. This is according to their brochures. The farm managers had had to work tons of lime and pulverized limestone into the soil to neutralize it, and for all this they needed a lot of labor, more than the profusion of old resident rednecks, crackers and pioneers our county could supply. So they brought in lots of labor. Black labor mostly.

The Palmers sold or leased out huge parcels - to the Chapmans, the Johnsons, and Thacker and Pearce - and all of them had to build camps for their workers. Lots of the jobs were seasonal, and migrants were hauled in from Georgia and Alabama. White labor recruiters brought in big crews. Black men of prominence with business smarts, like Elmo and Johnny Newtown, Nathan Coons, and Grand Pa Gordon were labor recruiters, too. A fair number of these imported working people decided to settle in our county. Early in the morning you could watch a parade of men and women walking to their jobs, from the camps or their homes in Bee Ridge. They'd come hiking along the railroad tracks, with their rubber boots and lunch sacks slung over their shoulders, reporting for work in "the celery."

On Saturdays, there was another parade, laborers from the camps hiking to the Overtown and Newtown neighborhoods here in Sarasota, where they could spend their wages shopping, eating and relaxing as much as they wanted because the law stayed away. Since the bosses couldn't lease out convicts anymore, field workers had become too valuable to arrest. Celery was the biggest crop we had.

About six months after I'd started drawing Palmer Farms checks again, the Chief Project Engineer Ormond Ludlow, who kept track of production figures, asked me to go out and see why the workers in "Section 3" were so slow. He was a smug numbers guy who had probably never left headquarters since he showed me around on my first day at Palmer Farms.

"How is that a security problem?" I asked.

"I'm just suspicious by nature," he replied. "Maybe they're drinking moonshine or smoking muggles. Maybe there's a labor organizer around. But check it out for us." He pointed his pen at me. He knew what "muggles" meant, and I didn't, so instead of sticking his pen up his butt I drove over to Section 3.

We were in early February, a time to transplant wagon-loads of shoots into the ground. The little green sprouts were set into rows that stretched to the horizon. There was a gang of workers, women mostly, bent over and sticking the little plants into the earth, and a platoon of youngsters carrying flats of the plants over to the women from three wooden trailers parked out in the field. I had to hike in a ways to get to them because I was afraid my truck would get stuck.

The trailers carrying all the plants had to be been hauled in by special tractors that had an extra tire mounted on each side to squash through the muck. My truck didn't have those.

The smell of the place was like a swamp, rich, rotten and wet.

Watching from the sidelines, the process seemed efficient to my eye. A foreman was on the job way down the row. He didn't seem to be the least bit curious about me.

It's a big sky out there, over miles of flat fields. Just a few clouds. You can't look at the sun, it's too bright. The farm is an endless carpet of black soil and brilliant green plants, and in the distance the field shimmers and sparkles, like looking over the waves of the Gulf of Mexico.

I didn't see any labor disruption.

The women didn't sing. They were ankle deep in mud. They wore dresses tied above the knees. Some wore jeans tucked inside their rubber boots. A brown bird dipped and fluttered on its careless flight over the expanse, but the women were determined to stick those plants into the dirt at their unwavering pace. I was conscious that I was just relaxing – leaned up against a muddy trailer fender watching a line of mothers dripping sweat off their faces, doing their jobs, while I was wondering what mine was.

One of the ladies straightened up and stretched. She was pregnant and wearing a blousy blue dress splattered with the earth she was seeding. Slowly she came unstuck from the mud and walked by me to go to the trailer.

"Sorry, boss man," she said. "Just need some water."

There were red sores on the back of her legs. The kind of sores that could come from fertilizer and celery juice daily soaking into the skin. Or from the lash of a riding crop or a whip. I nodded at her and watched her get a drink from a jug, then go back to her row.

"This ain't a bit different from the turpentine camps," I said out loud. "And I ain't no different from the Woodsrider." But not so loud that anybody but me heard.

I walked back to my truck and got it turned around on that narrow spit of dry land. At headquarters I handed in my Palmer badge to Kelsey, the man who had first recruited me for this part of my career. He was still around with some duties unknown to me. Quitting was getting to be a habit. But this just didn't feel like a job I wanted any more. The new director of personnel told me how to file for my last wages and get a check mailed to me.

So, now I was out of law enforcement one hundred percent.

CHAPTER TWENTY-TWO
THE PRESENT

This brings me all the way up to the present. Being a bachelor for so many months has given me time to think back on all those old adventures. That's the only good thing I can say about being alone.

Months have passed since Clarinda left me. I've had plenty to do to keep my mind off of her, but she is always there. I realize that I'm to blame for what went on with Estelle Braxton, and to blame for neglecting Clarinda – in the sense that I stopped taking a deep interest in what was on her mind. We had got married so young. Seems like a century ago. Neither of us had any experience in love. We just got married. Then there was building up the farm, and then our son Mack came along and had to be raised. And then here we are now. She left me without warning. I've had one post card from her in all this time. It's hard to forgive that, but I miss her very much. I stay confused about my feelings.

I'm trying to develop a more optimistic attitude since quite the jaundiced cynic I've somehow become. Being around law enforcement does that, but also seeing the timberland and cattle prairies of my youth ripped up for houses and the profit of developers. But there I go again.

I have observed good in people. Back when I'd go to church with Clarinda, I remember the preacher saying, "Let yourself be a reflection of the good." So, more confusion.

I went up in an airplane with my son. He flew over from Tampa and landed it right by Fruitville Road on a little airstrip the Army had built for emergency landings when it was training pilots in Arcadia for the last war. Once we took off, and after my fear of having a heart attack passed, I enjoyed the experience immensely. We soared out over Myakka Lake and the cow country I'd roamed when I was a younger man. Then came back west, over what had been pine forests but was now all getting chopped down for farms and houses. Flying over the Bay gave me the most beautiful view I've ever seen of the waterways and Gulf of Mexico, with sailboats and trawlers going about their business in every direction. Siesta Key had come back to life since the hurricane. We dipped down to scatter people swimming and fishing on the beach. And we flew right back over the middle of town.

Sarasota was quite the city now. Yachts surrounded the marina, and tall buildings were springing up on Main Street. This was the first time I truly realized how big it had grown. I suppose I was proud, too, since my life had taken me far with this place and deep into its life.

I noticed that in the metal box between our seats, Mack had stowed a Colt handgun like mine. I started to say "What the hell is that for?" but held my peace. Like father, like son.

Landing on Fruitville we taxied onto a side road and almost had a run-in with a mule-drawn wagon. Talk about a contrast. As soon as I got over the shakes this amazing voyage had given me, I asked Mack had he heard from his mother.

"She sent me a long letter a few months ago," he said. "It didn't have a return address."

"And?"

"She said she was fine, but most of what she wrote was about the beautiful birds she was seeing."

"Did she ask about me?"

"Not quite, dad. She said she hoped that you were getting along all right."

"Well, ain't that a piece of . . ." I caught myself. "Do you think she'll be okay?"

Wallace shrugged and said, "I guess mom knows what she's doing."

That's the kind of young man he is.

My friend Reuben Ephram's boat had gotten sunk in the hurricane, and he needed something to do to make a living. I called up Kelsey at Palmer Farms and told him about the situation. Kelsey had always liked Reuben, for the same reasons men usually did, and he took him back on. In fact, he gave Reuben my old job as Security Manager.

Soon thereafter Reuben called me up to say that they had discovered what was left of a body out near the Myakka River and the sheriff had been summoned to get it. Reuben had gone to see it, too.

The body was a woman's and had been there a long time. It was badly decomposed.

"One thing I thought you might want to know," Reuben said. "On her breastbone there was a carved amulet in the shape of a starfish. Seems like I remember you whittling such a thing one time."

"Doubtful," I said.

"Yeah, well anyway. She's unlikely to ever be identified," and he hung up.

That brought a tear to my eye. Seems Estelle never made it to California.

I knew it was her husband, Judge Braxton, who had done it. I dried my eyes and now my thoughts turned to justice, or was it revenge? How could I make him pay?

But pay he will! As the Scottish poet Robert Burns says, "They wasted o'er a scorching flame, the marrow of his bones."

Soon after his call about Estelle, Reuben came over to my house to see how his poor abandoned friend was doing. He brought along a bottle of brown spirits, bottled in bond, and we sat out on the porch to sip a bit. He let on that he'd learned where my wife was staying. She was in Pinellas County living upstairs from a ladies' sewing shop run by her mother, Lovelady Barlow. It was called "Miss Barlow's Needles and Threads."

"It wouldn't be hard to find her," he told me.

I needed time to let that information percolate.

I came close to unburdening myself of the information about Reuben's parentage that Missus Cordelia had laid on me, but I held my peace. That would have to wait for another time.

Not long after that, I was killing an hour walking down the street in Sarasota waiting while my car got its worn-out clutch replaced and who should I run into but Loralie Cay, the first girl who ever gave me sweet dreams, and she was as pretty as ever. We happened to be outside a restaurant and I invited her in for a cup of coffee.

We chatted a moment about this and that, and then she said, "I heard about you and Clarinda."

I didn't ask her how she'd heard that. Could have been anybody.

"You know I had my eye on you when we were kids," she said.

"I remember."

"I've got to say, Gawain, you look like shit."

"Wow. Thanks for that."

"I mean, you look tired and angry. And mean."

"Maybe I'm just getting older."

"Maybe. But what you ought to do old-timer is run, don't walk, find that woman, and bring her home!"

I had to go back to the farm and have a talk with my dog, Nero, on the front porch about Loralie's advice. I would never have expected her to say that.

It's hard for a man to go in search of a woman who has left him, and harder still to have to talk with her about what went wrong, and what could be made right, and what I should do better, or she should do better. Words you speak are never as powerful as the words in your head. But then I guess the question is, do you love her?

I'd rather stand up and face Billy Neal again, who, by the way, was the first and only man I ever killed, than struggle through a conversation about my relationship with Clarinda. But, for example, I'd sure love to have Clarinda here to talk to about my killing Billy Neal.

Nero is a good dog. But he'd feel the same way about me if I killed a hundred men.

I don't know what else I should do, sitting here by my lonesome. And yes, I do love her, from the beginning until now. I know damn well that convincing Clarinda to return to our life together is likely to be harder than bringing Charley Willard out of the wilderness. But I was just a young man then and hopefully the years have imparted a little wisdom to my hard head.

If I were a poet, my pen would write:

Clarinda, mistress of my soul
My life and light
The sun of all my joy
No other light shall guide my steps
Than the sparkle of you, coming into sight

So I guess instead of sitting here like a stump, I'll give it my best shot. And I aim to get her back.

THE END

Tony Dunbar has managed a deft blend of fact and fiction in his latest novel, The Story of the Sarasota Assassination Society. He paints a fascinating portrait of the good, the bad, and the ugly of Sarasota during its pioneer days, and it makes for a great read.

Jeff LaHurd, author of *Hidden History of Sarasota & Gulf Coast Chronicles*

The illimitable Tony Dunbar charges forward with another spectacular work, this time a historical fiction—a Southern, as this new genre is being called--about the most alluring of places, Old Florida. Lovingly researched and beautifully imagined, Dunbar brings to life a history that cannot stay buried, a moving and explosive story of murder, love, and redemption in the bizarre and rich landscape of the frontier. This fateful and gripping story is about the dramatic entanglements that kill us and those that save our lives.

Janisse Ray, author of *Ecology of a Cracker Childhood & Wild Spectacle*

Ever the consummate storyteller, Tony Dunbar power-dives into Florida history to produce a crime thriller that makes you want to say, "Wow! That really happened here?" Can't wait to see how the series unfolds!

Julie Smith, Edgar Award winning author of bestselling mystery series featuring *Skip Langdon* and *Rebecca Schwartz*.

Tony Dunbar is a Georgia-born Louisiana lawyer who lives in Southwest Florida on a tidal creek rich with leaping fish, herons, manatees and passing alligators. He is an award-winning author and, in addition to the *Florida Fables* series he has written extensively about Southern history and civil rights and is the creator of the *Tubby Dubonnet* mysteries set in New Orleans.